"THE BOSS" — a limited edition print by Michael Graham.
For order information on this awesome print contact:

Eco Enterprises
Box 10
Ovando, Montana 59854
1-800-458-2017

TREE STAND HUNTING

Paul Brunner

Additional copies of this book may be ordered from:
Paul Brunner
Box 10
Ovando, Montana 59854

$22.50 including postage and handling

Dedication

This book is dedicated to several people and, oddly enough, to a whitetail deer. To Jim Brunner, my father, and for thirty-six years the best friend I had in the world. He taught me an unending love and respect for the outdoors. The days spent with him with rifle, shotgun, bow, and flyrod in hand were many, but not nearly enough. Before anyone was using the word "conservation," he instilled in me a strong land ethic: a deep feeling of responsibility to nature and her creatures. Shortly after I scattered his ashes over the grave of his favorite Brittany Spaniel, the elk that cross our ranch to get to their feeding grounds changed their years-old route of travel. Their trail now goes over that grave. . . I'd like to think there is a message there!

To Gene Wensel, Barry Wensel, and Paul Schafer: true friends and the best hunters I have ever known. I thank them for their lessons in hunting, and more particularly, in bowhunting. Special thanks to Paul Schafer for teaching me that ethical bowhunting is FAR more important than a set of horns on the wall or your name in the record book.

To Karen, Tammy and Lad Brunner. Without their support, love, and tolerance I couldn't have written this book. Not only has Karen put up with my constant desire to hunt, she has been my hunting partner for a lot of years

5

and taken a lot of respectable "critters" with longbow and recurve over that time.

Last, but certainly not least, this book is dedicated to "The Boss" . . . . He won!

" THE BOSS "

Good Hunting,

Paul Brunner
"World's Shortest Bowhunter"

TREE STAND HUNTING

Table of Contents

Forward

The vast majority of my tree stand hunting experience has been in Montana. I have hunted from tree stands in the hardwood forests of New Hampshire, and have tree stand hunted in Canada and the South West, as well. The techniques described in the following chapters will work ANYWHERE with only slight modifications at worst. Even though there is a wide diversity of terrain, timber-types, weather, and feed from Canada to the Mexican border, the hunter is still after the same basic quarry ... a creature of habit ... a "critter" that CAN be outsmarted! Most of the examples, stories and photos are from Montana ... just take the example or technique, use your thinker, and put it to work in your area.

My reasons for writing this book are simple: I'd like to help other hunters (especially those who are just starting out) learn of the pleasures and rewards of hunting from above. This book isn't an "Ego Trip." I guarantee that you won't see this writer wearing tweeds, smoking a pipe, looking somewhat seedy and saying, "I've written a book, you know," at some cocktail party!

Two things have prompted me to write the book. One is that I am sick and tired of reading "garbage" stories in outdoor magazines about tree stand hunting written by "professional" writers who occasionally hunt. I have seen so much misinformation spread in these articles by so-called "experts" that I could puke!

The second factor that has prompted me to undertake this book is much more difficult to explain. Bowhunting is my LIFE! I feel a deep responsibility to my sport and to those who are relative newcomers to it. For the first fifteen years I bowhunted, I had to learn by myself. The mistakes I made were many and sometimes heart-breaking. I was very fortunate to meet three bowhunters about fifteen years ago who changed my life. They took me "under their wings" and taught me a world of knowledge about hunting in general, bowhunting in particular, and most important, about the ethics and responsibilities of bowhunting. Because they were so generous with their time and knowledge, I feel a strong desire to pass on those teachings and the things I have learned on my own over the past fifteen years.

CHAPTER ONE
Why Use a Tree Stand?

It's amazing how many bowhunters to whom one can talk and get the feeling during the conversation that this is the person who "discovered" hunting from trees. This seems to be an American trait and probably ain't all that bad. It's this brash approach to life that has made America the dynamic force that She has been for the last 250 years. One thing of which you can be certain, however, is that the modern bowhunter did NOT discover or invent hunting from above.

Since time immemorial, Man has hunted his prey from above: from trees, ledges, high river banks, boulders, and other natural high points. In many cases, the primitive hunter was forced to hunt from above because of the limited range and effectiveness of his hunting weapons; a club or fire-hardened spear wouldn't cut it at thirty yards! At ten feet, the hunter had a chance of getting food for survival. Even as hunting weapons became more effective over the centuries, hunting from above offered a tremendous advantage to the hunter/gatherer both in success and safety. In terms of safety, hunting from above was critical to continuation of the hunter's bloodline if the quarry was a grizzly, woolly mammoth, cape buffalo, or some similar nasty critter. In terms of success, hunting from above offered an advantage, since very few natural predators hunt from above and the prey's attention is usually focused on the ground around it.

Virtually any animal can be taken from a tree stand if you learn its habits and home range. This dandy impala was taken in South Africa by the Author over a water hole.

Why use a tree stand? The reasons are many and varied. As far as hunting the North American continent is concerned, the main advantage of the tree stand is the lack of tree-borne predators. We should probably talk about the whitetail deer in relation to predators, since that is the most commonly hunted big game animal in North America. The basic predators on whitetail deer are the coyote, bobcat, mountain lion, and in a few areas, the wolf. Black bears and grizzlies could be considered predators, but mostly on very young fawns. Oh yeah, let's not forget the biggie . . . Man! Examine these predators and you'll find that with the exception of man, none of these animals could be considered a tree-borne hunter. Until recently, the number of humans who hunted from trees was so small that it wasn't worth mentioning.

I never thought about it until Gene Wensel pointed it out to me one day when we were hunting together: all prey animals (those that are preyed upon) have their eyes on the sides of their heads. All predators have their eyes in the front of their heads. This is pretty easy to figure out once someone points it out to you. The predator's eyes are in front for the chase and for depth perception. The prey animal's eyes are on the side of his head so that he can take advantage of his peripheral vision and, hopefully, see the predator coming. Gene also made an observation to me that day over lunch; note where man's eyes are positioned on his head. We are predators. We're SUP-POSED to hunt! (This could be a dandy line to use on your wife if she's giving you a little too much static about your time in the woods.)

Because there are no tree-borne predators on the North American continent, prey animals use their side-mounted eyes for scanning the GROUND all around them. If you observe a big old whitetail buck walking through the forest undisturbed, you'll note that he is constantly scanning ahead, to the sides, and behind him. Most of the time, you will see his eyes pointed in one general direction, and his ears swiveling in those directions not covered by his vision.

It is probably impossible to be sure how many centuries have passed since there have been tree-borne predators on the North American continent. Suffice it to say it has been long enough so that the species we hunt have no inborn fear of attack from above.

Consider this scenario. The hunter is slowly stalking through the woods in search of a whitetail buck. Let's assume there is only one deer, the buck he hopes to find, within 300 yards of him. The buck is bedded with his back to the wind and his eyes constantly searching the areas not served by his nose. At the same time, his ears are constantly moving independently of each other to cover anything his nose and eyes might miss (Let's not even consider that uncanny sixth sense that deer seem to have when all their other senses fail them.) The first thing a deer (or most any other wild animal) sees is movement. Now, you can't stalk without moving, no matter how slowly you are still-hunting. Chances are pretty good that the buck is going to spot your movement, hear you, or smell you. Take a more typical case, and add a couple of does with twin fawns. All of a sudden you have fourteen nostrils, fourteen eyeballs, and fourteen ears that can spot you, and they're bedded far enough apart to insure that many different angles of approach are covered. Because they are in a group, these deer won't all have their backs to the wind. They will be bedded facing several directions, utilizing many noses and eyes as a team.

Sure, you can kill a buck in his bed, even with a bow! The last time I asked Gene Wensel how many deer he had taken in their beds with a bow, I believe he said eleven! Now that's an awesome feat, but Gene is an awesomely good hunter. He's one of the best still-hunters I have ever seen. He moves incredibly slowly and quietly. He makes sure that his clothing matches the terrain and vegetation perfectly. Most important, however, is that fact that Gene probably knows more about hunting whitetails than any man alive (with the excepton of his twin brother, Barry, who has an equal ability). Not only does Gene have YEARS of experience, he has a God-given feel for where the whitetail is and what he's going to do. This intuitive thing CAN'T be learned. Even someone with the talent for understanding the whitetail and the still-hunting abilities described above will tell you that you have a better chance of taking a deer, be it a doe or a Boone and Crockett buck, from a tree stand.

By allowing the deer to come to us, instead of us going to them, we have eliminated the main problem faced by all whitetail hunters — movement, the first thing the quarry spots! Let's make an assumption that is very important to your tree stand hunting, and one that will be discussed at length further on, in this book. Let's assume that you are able to put your stand up and enter it *without alarming the deer.* At this point, you are in an ambush situation, in a location that the average whitetail (or elk, mule deer, or bear) is never going to check out, AND YOU ARE NOT CREATING ANY MOVEMENT. You have a big advantage already. Now consider that in most cases of stalking, even if you do get close enough for a safe bow shot, the

Rob Davis with a dandy buck taken from above. Here's proof that smart tree stand hunting will take Big Bucks anywhere — this is from Maryland!

quarry is probably either aware that something is not quite right, or more likely, he's on "RED ALERT!" All of us who have taken a thirty-yard shot at a buck that is on "red alert" have had the sad experience of watching the arrow reach the center of the lungs a split second after the buck has moved them to another spot.

If you know your area, have done your scouting well, and have pulled a good "sneak" getting into your stand, the odds are much better that you will not be faced with a "red alert" situation. It's still a distinct possibility, but *better odds*. An un-alarmed deer walking or slowly feeding by your stand is a whole lot easier bow target than one that is tensed and ready to jump. They usually don't know something is wrong until the arrow has gone completely through them. The five of us who hunt together have all seen deer that have shown normal behavior . . . even grazing . . . after an arrow has passed completely through them. That puts an end to the Cleveland Amory myth that bowhunting is painful and cruel.

Quite often when Gene Wensel discusses hunting for deer that are un-alarmed in one of his seminars, someone in the audience will raise a hand and say that due to heavy hunting pressure in his area, there is no such thing as an "un-alarmed" deer in his hunting spot. The first bit of advice that any of us would give is to try to find a place where there are no other hunters. We hunt undisturbed deer here in Montana, because we go way out of our way to find private hunting spots. If that is just not possible, you still have an advantage if hunting from a tree stand. Your scouting will have to take into account that there are going to be other hunters in the area. Then you'll want to place your stand along escape routes or at the edge of the thickest security cover around. Most important in a situation where there is a lot of pressure, USE YOUR HEAD!!! Gene tells a story about the bowhunter he met, after a seminar in New Jersey, who set up a stand in thick timber at a wide spot on the median of a major four-lane highway! Seems the smart older bucks would head in there when the pressure started. They had feed, water, and never saw a soul. The bowhunter took a good buck there every year. USE YOUR HEAD! If the pressure is heavy, look for that little patch of security that no one else thinks is worth hunting; you won't be sorry.

Gene Wensel demonstrates the installation and use of a tree stand during one of his great seminars on whitetail hunting.

Since the ideal situation for any hunter, whether on the ground or in a tree stand, is an undisturbed situation, we'll assume we're hunting undisturbed deer unless we say otherwise. Given this situation, let's talk about the effects of wind on the tree stand hunter.

A tree stand hunter is no different than any other hunter with regards to the wind. You just can't expect a deer to walk into your stand from straight down wind.

The use of a tree stand *does* give you some advantages, however. Tests done with smoke grenades have shown that hunting out of a properly placed stand (15-18 feet high) will elevate the hunter's scent stream for a considerable distance before it drops to ground level. If you take this bit of knowledge, figure out the likely route of travel of your quarry, and take advantage of terrain, you have an exceptionally good chance of your quarry coming by your stand under your scent stream on the down-wind side of your stand. At this point, he is at least certain that there is no "smellable" danger and will be relying more on his eyes and ears. Remember, there is no fooling a deer's nose. Once he smells you, you're history. You may have a chance if he catches a slight sound or movement, but once he winds you, forget it. We have already stated that he's not likely to be looking up. Assuming you have a silent tree stand and perfectly quiet clothing, you should be able to draw and shoot un-detected.

Studying scent streams with smoke grenade in tree stand 13 feet off the ground.

18

I am never afraid to put a stand up on the up-wind side of a deer trail, *if I have to*, because I know what the wind is supposed to do, and I take advantage of it. Note that I said what the wind is "supposed to do." If there is a storm front coming through, and the wind is really "squirrelly," all bets are off . . . I use another stand location (usually one that won't work with our standard "wind out of the west" situation in Montana).

This is probably as good a time as any to explain something that I learned from the Wensel brothers several years ago. It will be an important factor all through this book, and hopefully, for the rest of your hunting life! First, I have to state that I am not a "natural" like the Wensels or Paul Schafer. These guys have some sort of "gift" for understanding nature and its "critters." I have to have it pounded into my head a hundred times to figure it out. One time after a hunt, I told Gene and Barry what I had watched that afternoon from my tree stand. Gene said, "That's your problem! You watched it, but you didn't SEE it!" Then Gene and Barry both went on to explain that a major problem of most hunters is that they will watch something happen in the woods, but not think it over, sort out what happened, and then store it in the world's finest computer . . . the human mind. Since that time, I have tried to SEE everything in the woods instead of just watching it. It has really helped my hunting immensely. It wasn't long after this lesson that I started taking big bucks with my bow. So remember, when you finally watch that big buck travel a ridge, SEE his behavior. Figure out WHY he was there at that time! THINK! Use your computer! If you watch a buck once and don't take him, that may be acceptable. If you watch the same buck in roughly the same situation twice, and don't at least get a chance for a shot at him, you are watching, not SEEING. If you SEE that buck twice, then you are developing a pattern. When you pattern a buck and use your head, he should be yours.

I much prefer a cross-wind situation, if I can set up that way. For one thing, there is a lot of deer travel that is done cross-wind or down-wind. For years I thought that deer only moved into the wind. When I became a *serious* whitetail hunter and started to see things in the woods, I found that this just wasn't so. Blasphemy? Not at all! Spend enough time out there and you'll see deer moving in all directions. Many times deer are forced to move cross wind or down wind by terrain, location of bedding areas in relation to feed areas, or a number of other factors.

Paul Schafer, second to none as a hunter, demonstrates that scouting and learning your hunting area pays off!

When you see deer moving without benefit of the wind, *generally* they will be younger deer that haven't yet learned to use the wind to its maximum benefit. You won't see many 8½ year-old bucks walking with the wind at their backs . . . they know better!

One occurrence that I had watched many times, but had not SEEN and understood, was buck movement in relation to the wind in the rut. Again, Gene Wensel to the rescue. (I owe this guy A LOT!) I mentioned to him that I had watched several big bucks over a period of a week of hot rut activity moving in what appeared to be a cross wind/down wind direction. I just hadn't been able to think this pattern out. I had seen it and could take advantage of it, but I didn't know the why of it. Gene's explanation was simple. If the buck traveled directly into the wind trying to scent a doe, he would be very limited because of her narrow scent stream. If he traveled straight cross wind, he would have a much better chance of running into her scent stream, but would lose the protection of the wind telling him of danger from the rear. By traveling at a cross wind/down wind angle, the buck takes advantage of wind notification of danger from his rear, and still has the advantage of the cross wind to bring him into the doe's scent stream.

SEEING these aspects of deer movement and behavior, and then knowing how the wind works for (and against) you, when you are fifteen feet off the ground, shows you one of the main advantages of the tree stand; height puts your scent above the deer's nose for a considerable distance. This distance is significant enough so that you can be in an ambush spot close enough to the deer's route of travel to get a good shot that you could NEVER get from the ground. As an example: you are fifteen to eighteen feet off the ground and twenty yards up wind of the trail he uses. His nose tells him that no one is up wind of him when he steps up onto the edge of the bench from

I designed this screw-in video camera mount to enable me to film my own "kill-shots". It worked so well, I started making them!

the swamp where he was bedded. He's really watching down wind... ALL his senses maxed-out! He's paying the *least amount of attention* to the area covered by his most reliable sense . . . smell. When he has carefully checked down wind with ears and eyes and takes his first step forward (now as relaxed as he's going to be) is the time to pick a spot and quietly draw and release.

A tree stand can give you a real advantage, when you understand the wind and how it works. You can use it as a tool to take advantage of the quarry's weaknesses (which may actually be its strong points, as in the example cited above). Every time you're in a tree stand, pay attention to the wind. Use a wind feather. We use a marabou feather tied to our upper bow string with six or seven inches of waxed dental floss. This way you can watch what the wind is doing from the stand. Observe the behavior of the deer you see from the stand. Are any of them smelling you? If they are, where are they picking up your scent stream? File this stuff away in the hair-covered computer.

To me, the third major advantage of hunting out of tree stands is observation. Because I am elevated, I can see more area that would otherwise be blocked from view by trees, grass, and brush. By seeing more ground, I can consequently see more deer movement. I can observe more

Observing from a tree stand allows the stander to see game movement not usually visable from the ground.

deer behavior; I can learn WHY they do things. One thing that I can guarantee you from personal experience; once you know WHY a deer does things, you'll be well on your way to patterning him and taking him!

Once several years ago I set up a stand where I had found a heavy deer trail coming into an alfalfa field. I was kind of surprised that the deer were coming in with the wind at their backs, but careful thinking made sense of it. The deer were bedding up wind of the field and no one had hunted the spot or even been in the area. The only human activity during the entire summer had been a haying operation conducted by the rancher. The deer were used to that and apparently felt unthreatened. Here I was with a tree stand down wind of the fence crossing they were using; what a set-up! The late afternoon I chose to sit there, I had over thirty does and fawns and a couple of "basket racked" young bucks come by me and mosey out into the alfalfa. Just before dark, I was glassing the meadow and happened to catch movement at the far end of the field in a little point of timber. Four really big bucks stood there checking the wind. Finally they walked out. All four were "Pope and Youngers." The following evening, I took the biggest buck with an arrow through the "boiler works." He went sixty yards and folded up. Because of the terrain around this alfalfa field, I doubt I would ever have observed those bucks and taken one from the ground. Because I was in an elevated position, I was able to see things not normally detectable and accomplished a goal.

Almost all of my pre-season scouting is done from tree stands or elevated vantage points. I can, just like anyone else, walk the edges of fields and read tracks. Once I've determined that deer or elk are using a particular field or feed area, then I want to visually observe them. Are there any big bucks or bulls using the field? How many animals

*Hey, these Wensel guys really know how to put it together when it comes to hunting whitetails from tree stands. Remember the name of this chapter, **WHY Use a Tree Stand?** Here's why!*

are coming in? Once I've found an area that I like, then I'll get quite a distance away in a tree stand, hay stack, the loft of a barn, or up on a hill and start using my binoculars. I want to study what's going on without any chance of spooking the deer. Unless the fields you are observing are perfectly flat, you'll see far more from above. Remember, that big old buck doesn't like being seen! He'll enter the meadow from a little low spot or from

Tree stands are great for photography as well as observation and hunting. This photo shows a camera mount we make for our Screaming Eagle tree stands.

a patch of brush. Chances of catching a glimpse of him are many times better when the observer is elevated. If you can observe him entering the field from the same spot more than once, that's the first place to consider putting up a stand. HOW to put the stand up undetected will be carefully discussed in another chapter.

Before I hunted from tree stands I was averaging about one deer per season hunting with bow and arrow. Since I started hunting from elevated stands, I can safely say that I have averaged about seven whitetail bucks per season and have passed up dozens of bucks each year. (Relax, I'm not poaching. We can buy multiple deer tags at the beginning of bow season in Montana.)

If you haven't made the move to tree stands, remember those three advantages: lack of tree-borne predators, playing on the wind, and scouting from an elevated position. If you have been hunting from tree stands but hadn't really given much thought to these advantages, make sure you DO think about them and understand them. Knowing the WHY of tree stand hunting is the foundation on which you will build your skills and success. These advantages are the first things you will need to file in the "hair-covered computer."

CHAPTER TWO

Choosing a Tree Stand

Because I am in the business of manufacturing tree stands, I was going to ask Gene Wensel to write this chapter for me. I really didn't feel comfortable with the idea of saying, "this is good and that isn't," mostly because I didn't want to be accused of pushing my tree stand and "bad mouthing" some other brand or type. I thank Paul Schafer for changing my mind about this. He convinced me to be honest and tell the story about how I got in the tree stand manufacturing business, and to just "tell it like it is" in regards to the good and bad in all types of stands.

My original tree stands were permanent stands; two-by-eights nailed between two trees that were from four to six feet apart, which were then planked with one-by-sixes. I killed a few deer out of these, but never a big buck. It seemed to me at the time that the big bucks figured these out in a real hurry. They were very visible to man and beast, especially considering that I had only been putting them about ten feet off the ground. Studies conducted since that time in Texas have proven conclusively that my observations were correct. Mature, smarter deer spot permanent stands very quickly and pass by them far enough away to render them useless.

Sometime in the early 1970's I met Gene Wensel on a plane. In those days, you could carry a bow in a case as

One of our original permanent stands. No cover and the bucks eventually avoid them.

carry-on luggage, and Gene noticed my bow, asked where I had been hunting, and we began a friendship that has grown over the years. It wasn't long after that meeting that we were hunting whitetails together, and Gene introduced me to the "portable" tree stand. Over the next few years we tried about a dozen different types and brands of portable tree stands. Some were outright abortions! Some were pretty good, but always seemed to be lacking something to make them "perfect."

We tried what are referred to as "self-climbers." One of Gene's favorite "sarcastics" when he covers tree stands in his seminars goes something like this: "I've tried a lot of different brands of 'self-climbers.' I put 'em up against the base of the tree, and no matter how long I've waited, I've never seen one of them dudes climb a tree yet."

For those of you who have never used a "self-climber," I'll describe how they work. You will also find accompanying photos which will give you a good idea of problems we encountered with them. Basically, the "self-climber" comes in two pieces: the seat section and the platform section. Each section has an adjustable strap that goes around the tree trunk. The seat section is just a miniature of the platform section and both work the same way. You stand at the base of the tree and put the seat section up against the bark and adjust the strap to fit snuggly around the trunk when the seat is in a horizontal position. If you put weight on the seat, it tightens the strap and creates a "seal" which then holds the seat in place. You then move the seat up to the head height and do the same routine all over again with the platform section. Now the fun begins! You place your feet in two "stirrups" on the platform section, and reach up and grasp the seat section. You pull down on the seat section (very much like chinning yourself), and while your weight is off the platform section, you point your toes down which causes the platform to tilt to a forty-five degree angle, which then breaks the seal. The platform section is now loose and can be brought up the tree by you flexing your knees and bringing them up toward your chest. Now, while still hanging from the seat section, put your weight on the platform section which (in theory) puts it back to the horizontal position and re-creates the "seal," which "locks" it to the tree. Now you are standing with full weight on the platform section and the seat section is about chest height. You tilt the seat section to a forty-five degree angle, move it up the tree to a height above your head and start the process all over again.

When we first tried "self-climbers," we immediately encountered a number of problems. For one thing, THEY ONLY WORK ON TREES WITHOUT LIMBS! There ain't no such things where we hunt! Now, one of the so-called advantages of the "self-climber" is that you don't have to use tree steps. So if you don't have any tree steps with you, how are you supposed to get up the tree to saw down the limbs so that your "self-climber " will work on

31

the sucker? (We all LOVE these products designed by heavy thinkers who want to make a killing in the business world, but haven't ever hunted enough to understand what works and what doesn't!)

At this point, we were all in basic agreement that the "self-climber" wasn't going to work for us but we had $160.00 sitting there and weren't about to give that up (these suckers are EXPENSIVE!). Once we found a few limbless trees, we gave the "self-climber" another try. In all your days, you will NEVER encounter a noisier stand! This thing sounds like the peeler in a log mill when it goes up the tree. At this point, Gene and Barry were rolling their eyes heavenward and cussing out manufacturers who didn't know enough about hunting to know the difference between "sick 'em!" and "fetch!"

O.K., now we're up about eighteen feet (and very

*Unfortunately, still pictures don't show movement. This "self-climber" has just slid about 30" down the tree when the man's weight was shifted towards the tree — definitely **NOT** safe!*

nervous), and we find the next design flaw. Obviously this thing had been field tested on a non-tapering telephone pole, but OUR tree (like most normal trees) had a taper to it, a fairly good one. Remember in the paragraph above how I described adjusting the "strap" around the tree trunk so that it fit snuggly in the horizontal position? Now think about this. If the strap is snug at the base of the tree and the tree tapers, what happens? You win the $64,000 question! The strap is loose when the stand (with you in it) is eighteen feet off the ground and the tree went from twenty inches in diameter at the bottom to fourteen inches in diameter where you are. The next thing you try to do (ONLY ONCE) is to readjust the stand with your right hand while you're using your left hand to hold the tree and fondle your rosary beads.

At some point, we finally got the stand settled into the tree. (If my memory serves me correctly, I think we ended up using tree steps to get it set up right.) The first time one of us hunted out of it was the LAST. The first problem encountered was when I got into the stand (using the tree steps) and turned to face the tree to hook up my safety rope. I made the mistake of getting close to the tree and my weight at the back of the stand caused the seal to break and the platform slipped about a foot down the tree. I was able to save myself by grabbing the seat section. Believe-it-or-not, I stayed in the stand and tried to hunt out of it for about an hour. It just wasn't a stand from which I could hunt! I didn't want to move on it. It was *very* unstable and noisy. If I can't move with full confidence in my stand with total silence, I'm not going to hunt from it.

If I sound sarcastic, it is because I intend to be. Ever since I began to buy my own hunting and fishing equipment, I have been getting "shafted" by manufacturers and dealers who are far more concerned with making money than they are in providing a well designed, quality product. If it weren't for a few companies like L.L. Bean, who DO take care of their customers and provide quality, I think I would have gone nuts!

Again, we began to explore the world of "portable" tree stands. One look at the "ladder" stands brought us into fits of giggling ... gimme a break ... do YOU want to lug eighty pounds of stand and ladder parts into the woods and try to set them up quietly? Next, please!

At this point, Gene discovered the "chain on" tree stand. At the time, the only company making them was the Loc-On company. Back in those days they called it the Loc-On LEM (the LEM was for light, efficient and manueverable). The Loc-On proved to be the best we had ever tried. It was carried up the tree by the hunter after he had installed screw-in tree steps, and could be installed quietly and quickly. All you did when you took it up the tree was flip the chain around the tree, hook it on an "S" hook, and set the stand by putting your weight on it. The stand, when properly installed, was very safe and stable. We had finally found a stand type from which we could successfully hunt whitetails.

I would guess we all hunted out of the Loc-On stands for about ten years with pretty decent success. We had our gripes about the stand and usually made modifications to them before using them. It was known to all of us that you had to stand rather than sit most of the time, because the seat was very low and made of canvas on a frame, like a hammock. You sat *in* it instead of *on* it. It tended to cut off the circulation to your legs in a short time. You couldn't shoot a bow from the sitting position. In order to stand up to shoot, you almost HAD to reach around and steady yourself by holding onto the tree or a branch. That created movement — and usually noise — at a critical time in your ambush. We tried to figure out ways to raise the seat, but the design of the stand didn't allow that modification; so we lived with it. There were other problems with the stand that caused us to miss chances at some real trophy class bucks, but none of us were mechanically inclined or inventor types and just accepted the fact that there was no "perfect" tree stand.

All of us noticed that in cold weather the platform creaked. The platforms were made out of plywood and later out of plastic. Because the frame was aluminum, which tends to twist, the platforms would creak in colder weather. We never noticed this in warm weather, say down to thirty-five or forty degrees. Once the cold weather came, you tried really hard to figure the direction from which that buck was going to come and plan accordingly. If he came from the wrong direction, and you tried to move, the stand would usually creak or pop and the deer would be gone!

Another problem we encountered was snow. The platform was always in the horizontal position with the Loc-On. It wasn't hinged so that it could be folded up flush against the tree. When you got into your stand after a snowfall, there was snow on the platform, and no amount of cleaning would get it ALL OFF. The minute you attempted to move to change shooting positions, the snow under your boots would crunch and your buck would go into "red alert" or leave the area. We tried everything to combat this problem. We tried carpeting the platforms. We tried rubber mats. Nothing really took care of the problem. Regardless of our complaints, the Loc-On served us well over the years . . . and it was SAFE!

At this point, I'd like to digress long enough to point out a few things. Let me again stress that none of us were mechanically inclined and had no inventive talents at all. We knew that the tree stands we were using weren't perfect but went right on using them because they were the best available. Maybe someday someone would come up with "a better mousetrap," but for now this was it.

About this time a really weird sequence of events took place that led me to design a tree stand; something I had long been convinced I was incapapble of doing. I had had a very serious parasite attack and had been under a doctor's care for four years with various problems caused by the aftermath of the "bug." The attack had left the chemicals in my brain in an imbalanced condition; I was having memory loss, lack of energy, and confusion when tired. (Relax, this ain't going to be the medical history of a hypochondriac.) The Doc decided to send me to another Doc, who could put me on this super special medicine. The stuff was pretty hairy, and a lot of "don'ts" went with it. The worst being no beer and no cheese. Imagine living for two years without pizza and beer . . . it's worse than a Stephen King horror story!

One of the interesting things that came of this new medicine was a subtle change in my thought processes. I asked the Doc about this and got one of those knowing little doctor-type grins. He said, "Yes, it's entirely possible that your mind will approach things differently, and you could notice changes in the thought processes." We now leave this boring program and go back to our main show.

All this took place in the fall of 1985; I found myself sitting in tree stands thinking about ways to improve certain aspects of my hunting gear. Up until this point in my life, I had been blessed with the mechanical abilities of a turnip. All-of-a-sudden, I began thinking of new designs for tree stands. I knew all the problem areas of tree stands that were presently available from spending THOUSANDS of hours in them in all months of the year. What was REALLY crazy was that I began to think in terms of engineering: how to brace a frame to avoid twisting, and how to design a much different type of frame for added strength.

One *really* nasty day of tree stand hunting caused the whole thing to come to a head. The temperature was twenty below zero, AND the wind was blowing! There had been snow the night before; when a real bun-kicker buck came by my stand on the "wrong" side, I tried to turn and take him. The crunching snow on the platform blew him out. I got down out of my stand, walked to my pickup, and headed for the local welding shop, which was owned by a bowhunting buddy of mine, named Howie Fly. I started drawing pictures on his welding table with a piece of chalk of the stand I wanted to build. This guy has known me for years and had real trouble believing that this was my idea. He liked to tell people that, mechanically, I wasn't smart enough to pour piss out of a boot, even if the instructions were written on the heel.

He showed me how to use the cutting torch and the mig welder, and pointed me in the direction of the scrap pile. About ten hours later, with lots of help from Howie, we had our first "prototype." We hung it on a tree outside his shop and three of us got on it (about eighteen inches off the ground) and proceeded to bounce up and down on it. It seemed safe, and the next day found me putting it up near a farm pond dam crossing. I liked it so much that I ordered new steel to be delivered to Howie's shop and became a permanent fixture there. Each time we would build a stand, one of us would come up with an idea to make it better. By stand number six, we had a pretty slick stand that actually looked good, too!

What I had made was a complete departure from ANY existing tree stand design, because there was an independent frame which paralleled the tree trunk. Then we added the platform to the bottom of the frame with a hinging mechanism so that the PLATFORM COULD BE FOLDED UP WHEN THE STAND WAS IN THE TREE!

This is a Screaming Eagle stand which is a chain-on stand. This stand has turnbuckles, which are an option used on leaning trees to keep the platform level. The chain-on type stand is the most stable and safest, by far!

This would allow the platform to be left up so that, even if it snowed, the hunter wouldn't be faced with the "crunchy snow" problem. After building the first one with a plywood platform, we switched to steel grating called "expandex." We did this to do away with the squeaking we had experienced in cold weather with plywood.

We made a nice roomy platform that eventually came out at twenty-five inches wide by twenty-four and one-half inches deep. We figured that a guy with size fifteen boots could turn in this comfortably. This caused our next problem: seat height. Although I wanted a higher seat than my Loc-Ons had, the years of tree stand use had geared me to a low seat. Because my platform was twenty-four and one-half inches deep and had to clear the seat when it folded, I had to make the frame long enough to put the seat at a height of twenty-five inches. It LOOKED too high! I tried the first one with the twenty-five inch high seat and it was perfect! It was really comfortable and you could easily shoot in almost any direction while sitting down.

Please bear with me on this story of my developing a tree stand. I am doing it for a very significant reason, because at this point in time, I WAS NOT EVEN CONSIDERING PRODUCING A TREE STAND FOR SALE! This was strictly to be for the five of us who hunted together most of the time. It's because the stand was originally designed for our personal use ONLY, that I feel I can objectively discuss choosing a tree stand.

I had made stand number twelve, when Gene Wensel came up for a weekend to hunt whitetails on my place. I sprung the new stand on him when he walked into our kitchen. His first comment was, "The seat's too high, but other than that, it looks really slick." We argued about the seat for a few minutes, but you never argue with Gene, because he cheats and becomes irrational. I dropped Gene off where I had placed one of the new stands and told him I'd pick him up at dark. When I picked him up, his *first* comment was, "Don't change that seat even so much as an inch! I've never been that comfortable sitting in a tree stand, and drawing the bow is a piece of cake!"

Seat height is extremely important. The hunter should be able to shoot any length bow while sitting. Note how well the hunter's clothing, especially the vest, match the tree.

Over the next month, Gene and Barry hunted with me and suggested changes that could be made in the tree stands. At their suggestion, I made the plywood seats padded and drilled holes that would allow bolting on a bowholder. At the end of the hunting season, the three of us were talking about how well the stands had worked. The three of us, plus two other friends, had taken nine bucks in the last seven days of hunting season; seven of those would have qualified for entry into the Pope and Young record book. The hunting conditions had been adverse in the extreme: as cold as twenty below, wind from the wrong direction, and snow almost every night. As we talked, Gene said, "That is the best tree stand that has ever been built! If you don't build them and sell them commercially, you're NUTS!"

I took Gene's advice just a week or so later. I brought my own wire welder, converted my ranch equipment shed into a welding and shipping shop and began producing and selling what is known today as the "Screaming Eagle Tree Stand." I named it that because of the U.S. Army's 101st Airborne Division, the "Screaming Eagle" Division. I liked their motto: "Death From Above."

I have told this story, as I mentioned earlier, for a reason. I apologize if it is long and boring. I wanted readers to understand several things. I wanted it understood that I never intended to be a builder of tree stands. It just happened when I came up with a design that has been called "the finest hunting tree stand on the market today." When Paul Schafer convinced me to write this chapter he said, "Tell the truth. Tell how and why you designed the stand. You're just as qualified as Gene to evaluate and fairly assess other stands. Just point out that you didn't get into this for money, but to build a perfect tree stand."

That's enough explaining and apologizing... probably

too much! Let's talk about what we have discovered over the years that a tree stand HAS to have and SHOULDN'T have in order to be a good hunting stand. If you are looking at tree stands there are several things that you can look for that will really help you in getting the right stand. I will list them in order of importance below.

Unconditional Money-Back Guarantee: If the stand manufacturer doesn't offer that, move onto the next one. We tell our customers that in addition to the 100% guarantee they can even try the stand out for a couple of weeks and return it for ANY reason. If the manufacturer has any faith at all in the safety and performance of his stand, he will offer the same.

Chain-On Attachment: If the stand is not attached to the tree by a chain, you are risking serious injury or death! This is not hawg wash, believe me. The stories we get from guys who have taken a fall out of "self-climbers" could fill a book. Some "chain-on" stands come with an optional rope (supposedly quieter). DON'T USE IT! They fray over time, and it seems that squirrels like to chew them. Some stands utilize a chain with a load binder to tighten it. I've used 'em and feel strongly that they are an accident looking for a time and place to happen. You can't beat a plain and simple and SAFE chain and "J" hook attachment!

Total Stability: When you're checking out stands, make sure the dealer or a friend who has one will let you put the stand up a couple of feet off the ground on a tree (some dealers have indoor display trees; they are fine if they are solidly mounted). Follow the mounting instructions and "set" the stand as firmly as possible. My first test would be to hold the platform in the middle of the outer edge with one hand and try to rock it from side to side. The stand SHOULD NOT MOVE! It should be rock

*Testing a stand for safety. ONLY a chain-on stand can hold
weight like this. The Screaming Eagle will hold 4,000 lbs.!*

*This is a pin-mount system. Slight hand pressure will pull the stand away from the tree and it will wobble like crazy. If it doesn't chain on, it **CAN'T** be stable and **QUIET**!*

solid. Next I stand on the platform and step out to the front of the platform and then to each corner. If the stand moves *or makes noise,* it isn't going to be a good hunting stand. I do the same routine on the back of the platform and then climb up on the seat! THERE MUST BE NO SIGNIFICANT MOVEMENT IF THE STAND IS TO BE CALLED STABLE!

Noise: The same tests above are used to check for noise. Noise in a tree stand is unforgivable and will someday cost you that record book buck! Test everything! Check for squeaking in the platform, check for any kind of noise in the seat. We tried one new stand that has an adjustable SWIVELING seat like a bar stool. This thing is a real joke; you can spin the padded seat just like the one down at "Frenchie's Bar and Grill," and it sounds the same, too! The guy who designed it wasn't a hunter; he was a BUSINESS MAN! When you have checked it out as outlined above, then stand in it in a quiet place, and

44

slowly turn 360 degrees and pretend to draw your bow. Test it the way you would use it if a buck came from the "wrong direction."

Ease of Installation: The stand should be light enough to carry up your tree steps to the spot you have chosen to hang it with no real strain. It should be designed so that it's easy to hold in place against the bark while you flip the chain around the tree and hook it to the "J" hook. You should be able to install the stand with a minimum of noise. I can now hang a stand (including screwing in ten steps) in under five minutes and make virtually NO noise. I learned a neat little trick from Gene: I dip my tree stand chain in liquid rubber. This worked so well for me that we now offer rubber-dipped chains as an option on our tree stands.

Ability to Hide and Lock: It's too bad this one has to be a consideration at all, let alone being important enough to write about in this section. Unfortunately, there are some MAGGOTS out there who use and/or steal other hunter's tree stands. Each year you hear more stories of stolen stands. Pick a stand that can be made just about invisible. Generally this means it will have to have a grate-type platform rather than solid. If the platform folds up, so much the better. What we do is fold the platform up, break off some pine boughs or branches, and put a few through the grating on the platform. With a folding platform made of grating, you can run your extra chain through the grating, back through it, and around the frame and lock it. Then the platform is locked in the upright position, AND the tree stand itself is locked. If they are carrying chain saws, you're shafted no matter what you do.

Fellow bowhunters getting hurt in tree stands freaks me out! If a guy is stupid enough to be in a stand without a safety HARNESS (more about that later) and gets excited

45

*With a folding platform made of expandex, it's easy to lock the stand AND lock the platform up. This stops the **MAGGOTS** from using or stealing your stand!*

*Hiding the tree stand is a **must** in areas where there are lots of other hunters. Expandex makes it easy to put branches in it, plus it allows light to pass through, leaving no silhouette.*

and steps off the stand, I have a minimum of sympathy. My daddy used to say, "If you're gonna be stupid, you gotta be tuff!" We've heard of several guys who fell asleep in their tree stands and ended up on the ground. Coffee and a harness will help this problem. If a bowhunter just

*Always use a safety **harness** not a belt! This one has a telephone lineman's rope on it, which is adjustable for different size trees.*

plain doesn't put his stand up correctly, that's his fault, too. What freaks me out is the stands that are poorly designed and are grossly unsafe. The manufacturer puts out a bunch of advertising in a reputable magazine, so the buyer assumes that the stand has to be good . . . .

The first year we manufactured the Screaming Eagle Tree Stand, Gene took them with him to display and sell during his seminars. He sold over five-hundred of them in three months, mostly in New Jersey and New York. Not long after that, I got a call from this dude from New Jersey who came on like a slick-o used car salesman. He told me that bunch of guys in his area had bought stands during Gene's seminars and really liked them . . . THEN came the pitch! It seems that all of the guys he had heard of or knew had the same complaint: the stand was too hard to put up! Now, I've put up thousands of tree stands in my time and I knew this was a crock! We were hearing how EASY the stand was to install from all the people who wrote and called. Anyway, it seemed that this slick-o dude had the perfect solution for the problem, because he was the sole inventor of the "PIN MOUNT SYSTEM!" According to him, my sales would drop to nothing if I didn't use his "pin mount system" . . . AND if another manufacturer used it instead of us, we'd be "out of business in no time!"

The slick-o from New Jersey sent me a pin mount and a special bracket to adapt it to our tree stand. We gave it a try. All you did was screw this thing into the tree and hang the stand on it . . . simple. When we gave it check number three (above) for stability, we just shook our heads! There was nothing locking it to the tree. Just touch the stand and it wobbled and pulled away from the tree. There was no way on earth that this mounting system would work in terms of stability and noise.

The next test we gave it was FRIGHTENING! We hung

the stand about two feet off the ground (luckily for me), and I climbed into it. I weigh 136 pounds. I stood on the outer lip of the platform and merely flexed my knees and lightly bounced. I did not jump, just bounced. The pin mount system pulled right out of the tree!

About a year after our testing of the "pin mounting system," I was flabbergasted to see that a "new" tree stand design utilizing the "fantastic pin mount system" was announced in a couple of the major archery magazines. I ordered one of their new stands that day (it took three months to get it). When the stand arrived, we put it up in the same tree and tested it. We got *exactly* the same results testing for stability that we had when we put the "pin mount system" on our stand. The noise tests were far worse because this stand had the adjustable bar stool-type seat that I mentioned before. I then climbed into the stand, flexed my knees and bounced as I had when testing

*The pin mount fails and the stand falls from the tree. The man in the photo **did NOT jump** on the stand; he merely flexed his knees and bounced twice. He weighs 189 pounds.*

the mount on our stand. One bounce pulled the "pin mount system" out of the tree, and I landed on my back with twenty pounds of tree stand in my face . . . got a dandy cut out of it, too.

This kind of poor product design has been a real heavy-duty problem for hunters, especially bowhunters. We find a lot of clothing and equipment on the market that has been designed by people who want to make a lot of money selling a lot of goods. These people are not HUNTERS and haven't the foggiest idea of function. One of the best examples of this is camo clothing. Most of it is made of a mixture of cotton and RIP STOP NYLON. Any guy with bowhunting experience knows that you can't hunt successfully in this stuff, because it's so noisy. The example cited above of the "pin mount system" is a whole lot worse. Not only is it impossible to hunt from such an unstable and noisy stand, but some bowhunters are going to be severely injured or killed in one of those rigs.

I've discussed the "pin mount system" at length for two reasons. I don't care if some readers think that I am "bad mouthing" a competitor, when I speak of it. A system as poorly thought out and as dangerous as this one needs to be exposed for what it is. The other reason for discussing it is to give an example of what we bowhunters face when trying to buy ANY product to use in our sport. Probably ninety percent of the stuff available out there is not designed BY HUNTERS, FOR HUNTERS. It's a very frustrating experience for the inexperienced hunter to spend hundreds of dollars on gear that he will ultimately find won't work for him in the field.

There will undoubtedly be more new tree stand designs coming along. Some will be abortions, and some will be well thought out and quality built by quality people who care about their customers. I would be willing to bet a significant sum that the ones that are in that second group will have been designed by hunters.

In no way were the writings above intended to sell you on any particular tree stand or stand design. You could very well try one of my stands, then try some other brand, and choose the other one instead. One piece of advice I can give (and I hope you will follow it) is to try several stands. The safest and the most sensible thing you can do is to try enough stands to be absolutely certain, in your mind, that you end up with what works best for you. If you're buying stands through an archery dealer, chances are excellent that he will hang three of four different stands for you to move around on. If you are dealing directly through the manufacturer by mail-order sales, remember my advice about the MONEY BACK GUARANTEE. If they won't do it, don't buy it . . . pure and simple! It is the ultimate test.

When choosing the stand, just remember the six test criteria listed above. Don't accept five out of six, either. All six criteria are important if you are serious about successful tree stand hunting.

CHAPTER THREE

Scouting

Scouting is, without question, the most important ingredient in the recipe for taking a big buck *on purpose*. I added the words "on purpose" to clarify something. Blind luck and perseverance will sometimes reward the beginning hunter with a really big buck where no big buck really should have been, or where no big buck should have been *taken*. We all hear those stories and usually get a twinge of envy. After you've spent a lot of time hunting and become more experienced, the challenge changes from that of killing a deer out of a tree stand to taking a particular deer. That deer may be a doe or smaller buck. That doesn't matter. What matters is setting your mind to take *that* deer, in *that* place, and at *that* time. You will have gone from hunter to selective hunter. It is usually at this point in your bowhunting life that you begin to SEE things, instead of watching things.

There are degrees of scouting. One can walk a fence line, find a deer crossing, and put up a tree stand. You do it knowing that deer cross there, but have no idea how many or whether there are bucks as well as does, and if there are bucks, what size they might be. You have a good chance of taking a deer this way, and *maybe* even a big buck. The odds are, however, against that happening, and the big buck wouldn't have been taken *on purpose*. I'm going to assume that the reader is either a serious hunter who is after a "trophy class" animal, or would like to enter that stage of tree stand hunting. With this in mind, I'll talk about serious scouting geared toward taking whatever would be called a "trophy class" animal for your hunting area.

We hunt BIG bucks! The reward of taking a big buck is really something. The reward in taking a BIG buck that you have come to know and understand is such a high that I can't properly explain it. To have "found him out," studied him, and figured out his "pattern" without him knowing you were there is the first part of what, for me, is the ultimate challenge. The second part of that challenge is then planning *successfully* how to take him in his own "living room." Believe me, that buck has a definite advantage! Proper scouting can, in most cases, tip the scales in your favor. Remember, though, in order to scout with the BEST results, you HAVE to make the decision to be "hardcore" . . . totally dedicated to your sport. (At this point, it's best to get your wife involved if you're married, either as a hunting partner or at least as a scouting partner. Making her your hunting partner is a lot cheaper than a divorce! For my lady readers, the same advice applies.)

For the rest of this chapter, and for that matter, the rest of this book, I'm going to assume that you are already "hardcore" or are willing to become "hardcore." I'm going to assume that your goals are the same as mine and those of my hunting partners: taking "trophy-class" bucks *on purpose*. If you're not going to be "hardcore" and have those goals, this book will still provide you with a lot of the "meat and potatoes" of tree stand hunting which should improve your hunting results. For those of you who want to go all the way, there should be some tips in these pages that will help you get that "hundred-and-seventy-incher."

I scout all year long. Almost every day of my life I am

involved in scouting to some degree. I scout in my mind as well as on the ground and from the air. If I am flat on my back with the flu and don't leave the house, I am still scouting because I mentally review things that I SAW in the field the season before. It's amazing how and when things "click" into place. One of the best scouting/hunting tricks I ever learned just clicked into my head on Christmas weekend a few years back, all because of a remark made by a rancher about the big bucks he was seeing on his place. (Read the episode of "Old Glassy Eyes" in the chapter called "MATCH THE NORMAL ROUTINE.")

Some mounted sheds. These bucks were definitely related. All four sheds were found the same day at a winter feed station.

Let's just follow the calender and I'll describe how I and my hunting partners do our scouting. One scouting method is the same no matter what time of year. Everyone drives a car. When I am driving somewhere, especially at dawn or just before dark, I am always on the lookout for deer that might be visible from the road. Some of the bigger bucks I've seen have been spotted that way. When I am out driving and happen to be going by a good looking piece of deer country, I'll stop at the ranch or farmhouse, introduce myself, and ask what their deer herd is like and if they allow bowhunting. Farmers and ranchers are some of the friendliest people on earth, if properly approached. I try to do this part of my scouting in the off season. Usually, the only time they see a hunter is the day before hunting season. (The hunter is always all smiles and friendship 'cause he WANTS something.) You would be pleasantly surprised to see how much more likely a farmer is to give hunting permission, if you visit him in May instead of on September fourth!

This buck was photographed while scouting a rancher's "stack yard" in January. We hunted him for the next 2 years until he was killed by coyotes in August just before losing his velvet. He would have scored well over 170 inches when he died.

These two bucks were photographed around stack yards, too. They are a couple of dandy bucks — "Keepers" in any hunter's book!

Scouting in January, February, and March is a lot of fun in western Montana. It can be combined with a lot of winter activities that can involve the entire family. Sometimes we'll just go into the deer yards looking for shed antlers. This is the best time of year to find them untouched by rodents. When you're doing this you see all sorts of things: plenty of deer for one thing, and lots of tracks. Sometimes we'll find a lion or coyote kill...if it's a buck that hasn't shed out, there could be a good set of rattling horns there. We've even found wolverine tracks while looking for sheds. It's always neat to find sheds. It really tells you a lot about the deer that have been in your hunting area that you never saw. "The Boss," to whom this book is partially dedicated, was only seen with his rack in place three times by hunters. The now-famous photos of him were taken by a non-hunting photographer after hunting season on a winter deer feeding station. When Barry Wensel came down to our place for a weekend "horn-hunt" and found the first shed horn from "The Boss," we were flabbergasted! Five of us, including the

The results of three days of scouting & "Horn" hunting in 1988. These trips produced several new tree stand locations and information on a couple of dandy bucks.

Wensels, had never seen him in a month of hard rut hunting.

You can be sure of one thing! Because of this "scouting" trip, there were five very hardcore bowhunters who were trying to kill that buck *on purpose*. In the next three years, the *only* one of us who got a shot at "The Boss" was my wife Karen. She found a scrape that she was sure was his and put an arrow about an inch under his brisket at forty yards the last evening of the season in 1983.

During our annual horn hunt in the spring of '84, Barry found this shed from "The Boss".

I've never met a whitetail hunter who didn't think that horn hunting was fun AND productive scouting. In addition to looking for sheds in the deer yards, we have an annual "horn hunt" each spring right after snow-melt. We go out of our way to make it a "family event." The hunting partners with wives and/or girlfriends show up on a Friday evening, and we have a gourmet game supper and a tiny bit of "firewater." We generally watch hunting

videos or footage we took the previous fall. The next
morning we all go to a winter feed station or to an area
where there is a deer yard. We set up assigned grid
patterns and cover them carefully. You won't believe
some of the horns you'll find. We also look for last fall's
scrapes, rubs, and any other important indications of
deer patterns. Some of my best tree stand sites have been
chosen during the "horn hunt." We have another multi-
course game supper on Saturday night and finish our
"horn hunt" sometime Sunday afternoon. One of the
things we all do while looking for horns is carry our bows.
This is a great time to use Judo heads and practice in the
woods. You aren't worried about spooking game, and you
can really have fun with some lighthearted competition
with your buddies.

One of the really big advantages of our "horn hunt"
scouting weekend is being able to discuss the sign you

*"The Boss" photographed in 1983 by Ed Wolff. An awesome
whitetail. His mounted sheds score 195⅝.*

find. There are a bunch of people walking around unconcerned about spooking game. You can look everywhere, even in the bedding areas. When one of us finds something of interest, we can all get together and compare notes on it. This has been some of my best learning time, because I can find a scrape, get Gene and Barry over to look at it, and we can squat down and discuss it. There may be quite a bit of argument as to which direction the buck was traveling, the number of bucks involved, and stuff like this, *but you have a chance to put more than one mind to work on sign interpretation.*

In April, May and June I begin to do my scouting a little differently. The green grass and alfalfa is coming up, and the deer are beginning to regain some of their winter-lost weight. In late April, in our area, even the bucks can be seen in the greening fields at any time of day. There is little or no *visible* antler growth, but a good pair of binoculars will usually let you spot antler pedicels. In most cases body shape, size, and "language" are a dead give away on bucks from three and one-half years old on up. Even with no visible antlers, it's usually fairly easy to spot the bucks.

Once the bucks have regained some of the body weight and the feed is up fairly high and loaded with protein, they begin to do most of their feeding just before dark and through the night. By June, on the mature bucks (three and one-half years and older) the new antler growth is in full swing. They will be working on Bez and Trez tines, and bases on old bucks will be heavy and impressive. The dominance the older bucks showed with full racks the year before comes into evidence again and is really easy to spot from a distance within a bachelor group of feeding bucks. I'll do a lot of driving around little-used county roads and farm roads in the evening at this stage of my scouting. The deer are pretty much unconcerned about vehicles at this time of year. (If they *are* concerned, it's a good indicator of poaching going on in the area.) If I stop the car, I'll do it slowly and behind bushes or trees, if possible. This is when binoculars or spotting scopes become invaluable.

In late July the bucks' antlers are getting close to full-grown — close enough so that you will know if a buck is a real trophy or not. (REMEMBER — YOU are the one who determines what is a "real trophy"!) At this point my general scouting tactics change pretty dramatically. Sure, I'll still drive the back roads looking over the farm fields and alfalfa meadows, but now I start a new program. If you have been doing your homework and doing it correctly, you're going to have a couple of spots where you have either seen good bucks or you're getting real strong vibes about what should be there. Maybe it's a spot where there was a dandy last year. At any rate, now is the time to start a new phase of scouting . . . .

A late July scouting trip turned up this buck on his morning visit to a rancher's salt grounds.

I always try to scout from above, from down wind, and FROM A FAIRLY LONG DISTANCE AWAY. The last thing in the world you want to do is let the deer know that there is unusual activity in the area. You want to watch and SEE what's there without ever alarming an animal. To do this, I will use the hayloft of a farmer's barn, a good, high hill overlooking the subject area, or a tree stand placed plenty high and far from the feed area. I'll pick a place (if possible) where I don't have to sneak in and out in order to avoid spooking deer. I have found the best time for scouting this way is in the late evening. I'll try to put in an hour or an hour and one-half for at least a couple of evenings each week per area. Dawn isn't bad either. If I can get to a high vantage point *while it is still dark* so that I can see what is leaving the meadows right at dawn, I feel I have a chance to see some of the bigger bucks that might have come out to feed after dark the previous evening.

Once I have located a buck that I would take if the opporturnity presented itself, then I begin to try to "pattern" him. At this point, my main interest lies with my quarry, but I'm still watching for bucks I haven't seen before. You would be amazed at the times you'll think you've seen every buck in the area, and all of a sudden some "hawg" comes strutting into the meadow — you can bet he is an old, wise, nocturnal buck, and you just happened to catch a glimpse of him when a whim brought him out early to feed. I have a rule that I pretty much live by. (It has also become a real CHALLENGE to me to make this rule work.) If I see a buck that I consider a "keeper" once, that's cool! If I see him twice, and PLAY MY CARDS RIGHT, I can take him! To let you understand that this isn't a super egotistical comment, let me say that I usually don't take him; I usually do something wrong and blow the chance. The point here is, if that buck has allowed himself to be seen twice or more, he isn't being as careful as he should be. If you SEE him,

63

and carefully catalog his behavior, and really study the area, you have a very good chance of getting a shot at him.

Once the hunting season has started, which is September in Montana, any scouting I do is done with bow-in-hand. I am hunting but I NEVER hunt without scouting at the same time. Through September and early October, the deer are not exhibiting any rut behavior to speak of, and are still utilizing farm and ranch fields or croplands fairly heavily. My main focus of scouting and hunting is travel areas to and from these fields, particularly fence crossings or other places where the deer are forced to follow some sort of a standard route (usually due to terrain or cover patches).

As the first noticeable rut activity begins around the tenth of October (in Montana, that's when we begin to see the first boundary scrapes and rubs along travel routes), I begin to shift my scouting and hunting focus to trails and places closer to bedding areas. IF POSSIBLE, DON'T GO

Hunting and scouting at the same time produces lots of bonuses. The author found this herd of elk in a meadow while looking for big bucks.

INTO THE BEDDING AREAS THEMSELVES. I'll scout around the bedding areas, reading the sign, which could be scrapes, rubs, droppings, tracks, or any combination thereof, and try to determine the travel routes in and out of the bedding area. REMEMBER WHEN LOOKING FOR THESE TRAVEL ROUTES, *ALWAYS* CONSIDER TERRAIN, WIND, AND NATURAL BARRIERS TO MOVEMENT.

When the first signs of rut activity appear, I have noticed that I start seeing a lot of bucks when and where I hadn't been seeing any (or very few). This flurry of activity generally doesn't include your real old-timers. What you're seeing is the younger bucks who may not completely understand what the rut is all about, but they know SOMETHING'S up. Not only will I see these bucks in morning and evening, but very likely they will pop up at any time of day, especially around mid-day. They are restless — the does aren't in heat yet, but it's getting close and these guys just can't sit still. I compare it to my teenage son right about the time he got his driver's license. He was as nervous as an old maid squatting in an asparagus patch! Once I see this activity begin, I am then scouting for three things: big bucks, does, and scrapes. (This is assuming I know the general lay of the land and the bedding areas.)

You're probably wondering, "Why is he looking for does when he has said all they hunt for is big bucks?" The answer is simple, find the does and you'll eventually find the big bucks. Everything in their chemical make up is now gearing itself for the rut — to the exclusion of *almost* everything else. If I am in an area where big bucks exist (I should be, having spent all year scouting in one way or another), and if I know the terrain, prevailing winds, and bedding areas, all I should then be scouting for is doe concentrations and scrape activity. If your scouting was done consistently, you should know where the does are.

65

Depending on the area in which you live, they may still be feeding in agricultural fields or they may have changed feed patterns. In Montana, the fields are all frost killed and the deer will have moved into the river bottoms for browse in November. Somewhere between the does' bedding and feeding areas or in those areas themselves, you should be finding scrape activity. The exception here might be in areas where the buck/doe ratio is out of kilter. If you have one buck for ten to fifteen does, you aren't likely to find many scrapes. The buck has so many does available that he doesn't have to use the scrape as an advertisement and pick-up point. In the area I hunt, our buck/doe ratio is excellent (about three bucks for every nine does), and the scrape activity is terrific!

Assuming you have doe concentrations and scrape activity and have it scouted out, you should then utilize your knowledge of the terrain, prevailing wind, and bedding areas to determine where your tree stands are going to be placed. We will cover placement of stands in a chapter under that name.

Scouting at the end of the season can be one of the best times of all to scout. In Montana that happens to be in December. The hunters have all left the woods, there is almost always fresh snow for "reading" sign, and even though the main rut is over, the does that didn't breed in November will come into a second heat (usually around the twelfth of December). This means the scouter will be able to observe some rut activity with bucks still carrying their antlers. In colder climates, the does are moving more in daylight hours and the bucks generally do likewise as they are now eating again AND looking for that occasional doe that comes back in cycle. An interesting aside here — last year I had the honor of hosting Leonard Lee Rue III at my ranch while he photographed deer. This man knows more about the biological lives of whitetail deer than any man alive, PLUS he's a fascinating speaker! I learned from Len that whitetail fawns CAN breed in their first fall. If the fawn is in excellent health and has been well fed, they can and do come into heat in December, after the general rut! So there is still likely to be some sort of rut activity in which you can scout for your next season's hunting.

One trick I learned from the Wensels in relation to December scouting is to backtrack. You are all done hunting, really not worried about spooking game, and in a great position to LEARN. Get out there in fresh snow, pick up a good buck track and spend several hours following him BACKWARDS. You will find it to be fascinating, I guarantee it! You'll see how he approached scrapes and rubs if he is still using them. Most important

Flying "The Mystery Ranch" just after sunrise (note the long shadows). There are three river crossings here on "Horseshoe Point." We've taken many fine bucks because of scouting flights like this!

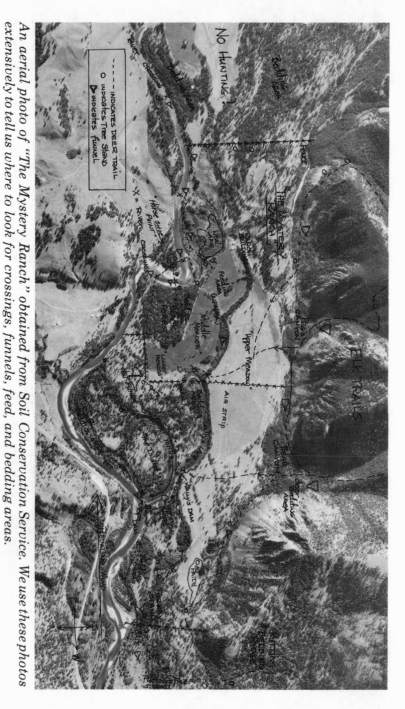

An aerial photo of "The Mystery Ranch" obtained from Soil Conservation Service. We use these photos extensively to tell us where to look for crossings, funnels, feed, and bedding areas.

is seeing what he does with his beds. How does he approach them? How does he leave them? WHERE are they? You can LEARN a great deal by doing this.

One of the best methods of scouting, especially new country, is from the air. Expensive? Sure, but worth every penny of the cost. If you figure out the cost of driving your pickup out to the farm several times, and then compare it to the cost of chartering a Super Cub or Cessna 182, you might be favorably surprised. If you hunt with one or more partners, split the cost and it gets pretty reasonable. Make no mistake about it, this is an awesome way to learn a huge amount of knowledge about an area and the game in it in a very short time. The best time to fly is right at daylight. The air is smooth and the game should still be out feeding. We have also found that deer are really visible right at sunrise because the sun hits them at an acute angle and casts long, easily seen shadows.

Some other things that we use in conjunction with flying are aerial photos and USGS quadrangle maps. We rely very heavily on these, ESPECIALLY if we can't fly the area. Most ranchers and farmers have aerial photos of their property and are usually very willing to let you look them over. You can also order them for almost any area from the U.S. Soil Conservation Service. Flying, maps, and photos will really show terrain and areas that we call "FUNNELS." There will be an entire chapter devoted to "HUNTING THE FUNNEL" further on in the book.

The decision is yours. Do you scout for a couple of days before the season and occasionally take a deer, maybe a decent buck? OR, do you scout all the time, whenever the opportunity presents itself, do you become "hardcore," and start consistently taking trophy bucks? I made my decision when I came under the Wensel brothers' influence — it was the best decision of my hunting career.

CHAPTER FOUR

Tree Stand Placement

The best hunter I have ever known when it comes to putting the tree stand in the "right" tree is Barry Wensel. This guy is uncanny when it comes to looking around, scratching his chin, and picking a tree. Even his twin brother, Gene, can't quite figure out how he does it. It is a blend of instinct and years of experience.

I can vividly remember a couple of incidents with Barry that are worth telling just to illustrate some points. I had hunted with Gene a couple of seasons before Barry came down to my ranch to join us in a weekend's hunt. The bucks were in the rut and there were about two inches of fresh snow on the ground. Gene and Barry arrived together with about an hour and a half of daylight left. I told them to get their wool clothes on, grab their bows, and I would take them out and put them in stands that I already had in place. Barry nixed that right away and said he just wanted to drive all around the ranch and see what was there and look over the terrain. We drove around a patch of timber that we call the Black Forest, until we came to a little point sticking out into the river that runs through our place. Barry told me to stop. He said he wanted to look at this little point, which was timbered and brushy and couldn't have been more than an acre in size. I thought he was nuts! Why would a buck live in a tiny patch of timber like that?

Barry walked over to the edge of the brushy point and got up on a tall old stump so he could look into the area without walking in. He spent a couple of minutes studying the area and came back to the rig, where he announced that a buck was using the area for scraping. He said he was certain it was a mature buck and could be taken just after daylight. We spent the rest of the time before dark scouting from the truck and letting Barry familiarize himself with the area prior to the next morning's hunt. Gene picked one of the stands I had

Barry took this buck the first time he hunted my ranch. His uncanny knowledge of whitetail let him predict the kill.

already put up, and Barry decided to hunt from the tall stump over-looking the brushy point. Barry left the house on foot the next morning about forty minutes before daylight, so that he could be on his stump a little before dawn. Ten minutes after legal shooting light, a nice 5x5 walked into a scrape about twenty-five yards from Barry. If you are a mature whitetail buck with a good rack, one thing you NEVER want to do is get within thirty yards of Barry Wensel — it is sure SUICIDE! Barry center-punched that buck with his Schafer Silver Tip Recurve!

Another time, Barry came down to hunt with me, and I took him to a neighbor's ranch where we had permission to hunt. This was in an archery-only area, and we each had five extra either-sex deer tags. It was noon and the rancher had been cutting firewood in the area. We felt nothing would be screwed up if we went in and looked the area over and checked out the stands I already had in place. In one area along the river, I showed Barry where I had a stand near the river bank and below a high bench. I was certain that the bucks traveling that area would be down in the thick brush rather than up on the open bench. Barry spent about two or three minutes looking over my stand and the lay of the land. He then got one of those "I know something that you don't know" looks in his eyes and took off up the hill to the rim of the bench. The bench overlooked the river and about a mile of open sagebrush. Barry asked me if the deer in the area used the sagebrush for feeding and bedding. I told him that they used it a lot, which was one of our problems in this area. You could see some dandy bucks out there in the sage but couldn't get within two hundred yards of them before they had you pegged.

Barry looked around and pointed to a lone ponderosa pine tree on the edge of the bench and said that's where he would put a stand. I couldn't believe my ears. All the years of teaching from these two guys told me to be down in the

Barry's all time best — "Old Hoss". Taken from a tree stand, B & C score 2016/8. Will he ever top this one? "Only the Shadow knows."

brush on the river bank. The bucks should move through the thick stuff, not the open! Barry said that NORMALLY this would be the case, but he just had a gut feeling about this. He explained that because of the size of the open sage area, a buck would rely more on vision to locate an estrus doe than on scent. At the same time he could be near thick cover or the safety of open cover, while being able to scent check and visually check the river bottom thickets. I knew enough to follow Barry's hunch and immediately went down, pulled my stand and steps, and came back up on the bench, hung the stand, and cut my shooting lanes. In the next five days, I shot three whitetail bucks from that tree stand: one spike and two bucks in the 130-137 inch class. What is even more interesting, is that I changed another stand about a mile away that was in exactly the same kind of set up. I put an acquaintance in the newly moved stand and he arrowed a whitetail that scored 154! The night after that, Gene got in the same stand and took a 5x5 buck that scored 126!

Placement of the tree stand in the area that you have chosen to hunt is a critical part of taking the deer that you have spent so long in scouting. Traveling around and doing seminars, I hear countless stories from guys who have really done their homework all year long, put up their stand, and had the buck walk buy *just* out of range. Placement of the stand is also the most difficult part of tree stand hunting to teach or explain. Successful tree stand placement is largely a function of experience, of *hundreds* of attempts and failures mixed (you hope) with some successes, too.

The best advice that I can give, is to think like a buck! Let's assume that you really did a super job of scouting. You've found a buck that you would take (maybe there are a couple of keepers in the same general area), you have really studied the terrain and prevailing winds, know the bedding areas and the location of does and scrapes.

Where do you put your stand? For one thing, I use more than one stand. Even though I use portable stands, I don't want to be out there constantly moving them — the less disturbance, the better. There are other important reasons for using several stands. I like to hunt near the bedding areas in the early morning. In the middle of the day, I might hunt a trail area where deer may pass going from one area to another. In the evening, I definately want to hunt near scrapes and where the does and fawns are likely to come out to feed. I also try not to hunt the same stand two days in a row, if I can avoid it.

One of the problems that we encounter in Montana is unexpected changes in wind direction, which can really foul you up, or a complete lack of ANY wind. (I love it when THAT happens!) These are more reasons for having more than one stand up. Nothing torques me more than having the wind change during the night and not having an alternate stand from which to hunt! I have one location where I put a stand every year along a bench above a great bedding area. For a number of reasons, this stand CANNOT be used if there is ANY air movement at all. When there is absolutely no air movement, this stand is so productive, that it's spooky. I have to go into it THROUGH the bedding area at least an hour before daylight to get into the stand. From fifteen minutes before shooting light until around 9:30 a.m., deer are moving in all directions. Two main trails into the bedding area come together about thirty yards from my stand, and a heavily used scrape line runs along the edge of the bench which overlooks the thick brush along the river that the deer use as their bedding area. When there is no air movement the deer can't pick up my scent anywhere (two years' experience has proven this, although I am certain to use an appropriate cover scent for the area), and they don't follow any particular movement pattern. It's quite common for bucks to come OUT of the bedding area as well as go into it. It's been my observation that this happens right after first light, so it's a safe bet to assume that they go into the bedding area looking for does and then out again to check the bench for does on the way into the bedding area.

This is where thinking like a buck comes into play. I try very hard to put myself in his hooves. I try to take thirty years of MISTAKES and weed out all the things that could help me in today's situation. (Notice that I said

Mark Mitten with a huge Illinois buck taken from a Screaming Eagle tree stand. Scouting and correct tree stand placement pay off!!

"MISTAKES." Mistakes are what make up experience, much more so than successes, which are much less frequent in hunting!) I try to compare the behavior of the buck I am after with behavior of previous bucks I have hunted. I then try to match terrain, wind, and other factors with similar past situations. This USUALLY gives me an idea of how to go after my quarry. I begin to think like the buck and feel what his route is likely to be (if he is undisturbed), where he is likely to be most alert, and where he is likely to be least alert. Once I have established what I think his undisturbed route will be, I then begin looking for the perfect place to put a tree stand.

The most likely place for me to try to find for my tree stand will be a bottleneck or "funnel." This is one of the greatest tools in whitetail hunting (or any other animal, for that matter). On one hand, the quarry is very likely to be much more cautious than if he were in thick brush, but on the other hand, he HAS to go through the funnel area. If I can, I will place my tree stand somewhere on the approach to the funnel or somewhere on the funnel exit. I generally prefer the exit end of the funnel (ASSUMING THE ANIMAL IS MOVING IN THE DIRECTION YOU EXPECT HIM TO BE), because the animal has moved through the area of potential danger and is likely to go back to normal-alert situation rather than the hyper-alert mode you can expect in the area in which he is *forced* to travel due to terrain.

A couple of good examples of what I'm talking about here would be a river crossing or a dam. If the river is fairly good sized, the deer will cross in riffles if undisturbed. Many times I have watched deer come to the edge of brush on a trail leading to a river crossing, and stand just inside the brush watching. When they are crossing the riffle, their attention is largely focused on their footing but you can't hang a stand in the middle of the riffle (lack of trees) and shouldn't shoot at animals in the water anyway (lack of fair play). The logical place for a tree stand, if the wind permits, is just inside the timber or brush on the exit side of the crossing. When the deer enters the brush, he will go off his hyper-alert mode. A dam crossing, such as a farm pond, beaver dam, or large reservoir is similar. With a dam, there is good likelihood that there will be a tree somewhere close enough to use. The question is, should you use it? I would still go for the exit side, if wind and cover allowed. If animals are traveling a funnel in both directions, I get far enough into the cover at the edge of the funnel to get a shot when the critter should be out of, or not yet into, the hyper-alert mode.

If there is no bottleneck or funnel situation, or if there is, but it is not usable due to wind direction, then you are forced to really use your thinker. This is where the importance of prior experience enters into the picture. Even if you can think like your quarry, you will have to make a lot of mistakes before you begin to "get it together" with any degree of consistency.

If I am going to set up my tree stand on a trail, be it just a deer trail, or a scrape or rub line, I'll always try to set up on a bend in the trail if possible. On a straight stretch of trail a deer is much more likely to be looking around and ahead. On the bend, his attention is more likely to be on the ground in front of him. He is also likely to be looking toward the *outside* of the bend, because he is facing the outside. Because of this, I always try to set up on the inside of the bend. If I have to set up on a straight section of trail for one reason or another, I'll try to set up in a tree with plenty of cover branches. I will also try to have three or four trees in front of my tree and the same behind me to serve as cover. I make sure I cut shooting lanes so I can have the opportunity to shoot in several directions. These lanes will also help me to spot a deer coming down the trail in time to get my bow ready if it looks like a shot might be taken.

I hunt in one place where the deer use trails a lot. Even the larger bucks will use these trails, because they are in some really thick brush in an area that receives very little hunting pressure. On this particular property we have a really predictable west wind. What I looked for on this property were trail *junctions*. I knew I could set up down wind and rarely encounter an adverse wind situation. I chose trail junctions because I doubled or tripled or quadrupled my chances by being where multiple trail use could bring almost any moving deer by my stand. Over the years I have hunted these same junctions again and again. I don't hunt the same stand every day and usually move my stand at the beginning of each hunting season to keep the deer from getting tipped-off to the stand location. Sometimes I'll move the stand part way through the season, but that is usually done if I notice a fair amount of buck movement that is just out of my effective shooting range. When hunting out of a tree stand, I prefer shooting at ranges of twelve to twenty-five yards, although I have taken deer at forty to fifty yards from a tree stand on occasion.

I try never to pick a tree that is literally right at the edge of a trail or a route I expect a buck to take. Generally I will pick a tree that is fifteen to twenty-five yards from the trail. There are several reasons for this. The most logical is the possibility for the buck to see or hear you when you move to shoot or start your draw. One other less obvious reason is that I don't like to shoot straight down at an animal or at too sharp an angle. I would much rather have that fifteen to twenty yard shot and have a better angle. It gives you a lot more of the "boiler works" as a target, and you don't have to hold quite as low. Another important reason is scent. If a buck walks right by the base of your tree he is much more likely to catch a slight whiff of where you put your bow down, etc., than if he walks twenty yards from your tree.

Probably one of my favorite set ups, and one that we don't seem to find too often, is what I call the "tight cross wind" set up. There is a fair amount of risk in this kind of a tree stand set up, but IF everything goes right, this is one of the most productive set ups I know. If you can find a heavily used trail or some sort of a funnel situation where the wind is STEADILY blowing at a very slight cross wind to the trail, you may be in for some exciting hunting. I found a REALLY THICK beaver swamp one time where three big bucks were bedding. They were only about 150 yards from an irrigated alfalfa field that was directly up wind of their bedding area. I watched them from a hay shed several times and had just about given up on them due to the wind, but decided to check the situation out anyway. I waited until mid-day and drove my pickup right into the meadow just the way the rancher would have (I made sure I had permission first). I walked over to the edge of the swamp with my bow in hand and held it up to watch my wind feather and see what the wind was doing. The wind was NOT blowing right at the bedding area! It was blowing just a few degrees to the north of the trail! I quickly and quietly put up a stand and slammed the door of the pickup (just like the rancher would have done) and drove away. The next afternoon I walked through the hay meadow to my stand a full two hours before I expected the deer to come out to feed. By the time the shadows were getting long I heard light splashing noises behind me as deer came through the swamp. The "troops" began to arrive. The first doe and twin fawns came out with only minor scrutiny of the field — THEIR NOSES TOLD THEM EVERYTHING WAS O.K.! After that, each deer coming up out of the swamp would see deer already grazing and would undoubtedly have heard the deer moving through the swamp with no alarm snorts. After eighteen or twenty does and fawns were in the field I heard more splashing and very carefully looked behind me to see a great big rack coming through the thick willows. The buck came to the edge of the swamp, looked out at the feeding deer, and started to saunter out to feed. I brought my Schafer recurve to full draw, picked a spot just behind his foreleg, and released as I hit anchor. The arrow went cleanly over his back and deer exploded in every direction. Right stand placement, but crappy shooting!

One thing that I do every summer is check with all the ranchers on whose ranches I hunt and find out what crops are being planted in an area where most every agricultural field is alfalfa or grass hay. Usually, a rancher will plant a crop in a year when he decides one of his hay meadows is thinning out and had to be re-seeded. Here in Montana, often as not, that means oats, and our deer go BONKERS over the occasional oat patch! If I can find an oat patch, I'll go check it out for an early September stand location. (The ranchers usually harvest the oats sometime in mid-September or turn cattle in on them.) What I look for is the deer trail that enters the oat patch from a cross wind angle or that rare case where the deer come in from up wind. I'm looking at a field right now that I know will be in oats this summer. It parallels a BIG river which runs due south. The wind is straight out of the west and the deer will HAVE to come out of a bedding area south of the field, come down off a bench, and cross a fence. I'll set up on the fence line somewhere and know that, *in terms of the wind*, I'll be in the PERFECT set up.

One thing that I learned from Gene that I feel is very important is the actual placement of the stand in the tree. In my early years of tree stand hunting, I would sometimes be real uncertain as to which tree in a general area to use. Gene came along and pointed out that for my own psychological well-being I needed to be *certain* that a particular tree was the right one. If I climbed in a tree stand and immediately began to wonder whether I should have put the stand "over there," I wouldn't have that total confidence which is necessary to do the job right. I now plan *from the ground* which way my platform will face and roughly how high I want the stand. (You may find that it will need to be higher or lower for better hunter visibility once you get up to approximate stand height.) I generally try to place my stands between fifteen and eighteen feet from the ground. One of my hunting partners prefers his stand height to be about ten feet. Although I feel this is too low, I do believe that each hunter should do what is best for him or her. I usually use around nine steps, so I always carry ten with me. If I don't use all ten, then I have an extra one that I screw in about shoulder height on my left side. I hang my camera from it. You can get some really neat pictures from a tree stand.

In this chapter, I've sat and gnawed my knuckles over discussing the placement of tree stands. It is, without question, just about the toughest thing to teach anyone. I even find it difficult when the learner is right there with me on the ground! The reason is quite simple, and I've mentioned it previously. Correct tree stand placement is largely learned by trial and error over a long period of time. You might learn quite a bit from two or three successes, but most of your real heavy-duty learning will come from HUNDREDS of failures — MISTAKES! Believe it or not, I actually LIKE to make mistakes! Oh sure, I am really torqued at the time, but I am pretty stubborn, and I find I REMEMBER better when I have made a really stupid mistake. My pride gets to working overtime, and I make darn sure that the same mistake doesn't happen again. I have a great deal of respect for the hunter who comes in after the hunt and discusses a mistake that cost him a big buck and mulls the whole thing over before installing it in the hair-covered computer. My respect lessens if the guy pulls the same mistake a second or third time. It usually means he isn't SEEING but only watching, or he's just plain stupid.

REMEMBER, in theory, YOU are smarter than any game animal, even the whitetail deer. You have to THINK when you hunt. You have to THINK about every hunting experience you have ever had and put it to work for you. Then you have to try to THINK like your quarry, which is a creature of habit with far better senses than yours. You are pitting your superior brain against his inferior brain but against his superior senses in his "living room."

CHAPTER FIVE

Hunting the "Funnel"

Hunting the "funnel" has changed my whole hunting life. In my opinion, it is the single most productive technique there is for consistently taking trophy animals. I have used it with tremendous success on whitetails, elk, mule deer, and bears while hunting from tree stands. I have yet to find a place that didn't have all kinds of natural funnels. They are everywhere in nature. There are also man-made funnels and since I have learned how to create them, I have been able to make game animals do what I WANT them to do instead of being at the mercy of their travel patterns.

The funnel is just what the name implies. It is ANY ONE OF DOZENS of natural barriers that cause game movement to "funnel down" into a particular area. The list is almost inexhaustible, going from the super obvious to the least noticeable (some funnels exist only in the minds of big, old bucks, and aren't even there for younger bucks or does). Let's go through a *partial* list of some common natural funnels. As I sit here writing this, I will create the following list from memory of actual funnels that I have found and used while tree stand hunting.

River Crossings: Look for the shallow riffles in any stream that has a fair volume of water or has deep holes. If a particular riffle is a heavily used crossing, there will

Gene Wensel with a nice whitetail taken in a "funnel" along a river.

be a definite trail leading to it. I have seldom found two heavily used crossings within a hundred or two hundred yards of each other. This is a perfect funnel.

Dams: Any kind of a dam, be it a farm pond dam, beaver dam, reservoir dam, or even the shoreline of a lake, will make a good funnel, if the water behind it is deep enough and covers enough travel route to force the deer across the dam. We frequently see this on beaver dams, ESPECIALLY WHEN THE BEAVER POND IS FREEZING OVER, BUT THE ICE WON'T YET HOLD THE DEER! Remember those capital letters!!! This rule applies to water bodies where deer cross the water as often (or more often) as the dam. Once the ice forms, the deer won't use it until it will support their weight. Some places we hunt, in this category, are only good funnels for a week or two, but during that time they are DYNAMITE!

Ridge Lines: Often times, we will find that a ridge line can create a natural funnel. The funnel will not always be in the same place — that depends on the shape, height, and direction of the ridge. There are always a bunch more factors, too. How steep is the ridge? How open or thick? At any rate, always check around ridges for trails that would indicate that the terrain is somehow creating a funnel. Check the ridge top, sides, slight depressions or deeper draws, and the base of the ridge for patterns of deer movement, where some factor of terrain or security is funneling their movement.

Cliffs, Ledges, and Mountain Sides: We hunt one ranch with a really high mountain coming right down to the ranch bottom ground, where the meadows and brushy bottoms are. There are two canyons where the deer can go up the mountain, the rest being sheer six-hundred foot cliffs. At the base of the mountain there is a border of trees and brush that is only about sixty yards wide in most places. This is an excellent funnel for whitetails, elk, some

Matt Riley, one of our hunting buddies from New Jersey, checks out sign on a dam. There is another large body of water just beyond Matt. We put stands at each approach to this dam, and one in the tree to Matt's left. Did it work? Does Howdy Doodey have a wooden fanny?

A heavily used deer trail crossing a creek and then a riffle in a large river beyond. A natural funnel that is a dynamite spot to nail a big buck.

*It's hard to see in a photo, but this is a **heavy** trail used by whitetails and elk to cross a riffle in a large river. The wind is **always** 90° cross wind on this trail. It is the* **Perfect Natural Funnel!**

mule deer, and even black bear. The two canyons are also total funnels, but because of strong down drafts in the morning and up drafts in the evening, can seldom be used for funnel-type ambushes. We always leave a stand somewhere on each of the canyon trails in the event there is no wind or some fluke cross wind. Not too many years ago my wife, Karen, sat a tree stand one evening in one on these canyons when the breeze was a down draft. She was waiting for a big buck that was bedding up the canyon to come into the hay meadows. Shortly after taking her stand, she saw a real nice black bear coming down the trail and slid one "through the boiler works" at twelve yards — her first bow kill!

River Edges: River banks and lake shores are some of the best funnels throughout the United States. Even in the flat lands, where funnels like those above don't occur, there always seems to be some major body of water near

Karen Brunner with her first bow kill — a dandy Black Bear taken from a tree stand in a canyon — a natural "funnel".

good whitetail habitat. Many times, while scouting new potential hunting territory, the first place I will check for major travel routes is along the bank of a river, swamp, or large pond. THESE TYPES OF FUNNELS REALLY GIVE YOU A CHANCE TO USE THE WIND TO YOUR ADVANTAGE, because of the meandering nature of shore lines. It's a rare river that runs arrow-straight for miles. Once I find a river bank trail, I look for the bend that will allow me to set up in a cross wind situation. REMEMBER THIS TOO: most agricultural development along water leaves timber and/or brush between the field and the water. This timbered area is the "safe" area, in which deer (especially big bucks) like to travel. This is one of the most common and best funnels throughout the country.

A good heavy buck taken by the author on a ridge with a natural funnel set up. The deer had to use the center of the ridge for movement to a feed area.

One of the best ranches that I hunt has been heavily logged all along the river, which runs through it for about six miles in a general north to south direction, although there are dozens of river bends. The trail network along both river banks is mind boggling with about ten heavily used crossings on wide riffles in the river. The prevailing winds are almost always out of the west. During the rut, buck movement can occur all day long up and down the river. There is enough room for five or six bowhunters to work the twenty-odd stands we put up each year without alerting the deer to what is coming down. We really score on this place during a really hot rut period.

Wherever you can find a narrow strip of timber along a body of water, SCOUT! Also, take note of ANY feature that will force the deer to use the shore line for travel. It might be a ridge or steep hill coming down to the water's edge, fields, buildings, or even a road. The river, lake, or

Ron Frahm with an Iowa buck. Here's what Ron says, "I hunt various timbers along the Little Sioux River in northwest Iowa. I like to hunt bottlenecks, or areas where different edge structures meet to funnel deer past my stands."

This is the gate that all the elk were using going from feeding to bedding urea. Look carefully and you'll see the hunter in the tree stand. A gift from Heaven!

swamp shore lines are super places to look for scrapes and rubs during the pre-rut and general rut activity periods.

Fences and Gates: We hunt these funnels primarily in our September season, because the crops are still green, and deer and elk are using these meadows pretty heavily. In an area where there are elk feeding, this type of funnel works really well because they generally raise hell with fences and will have their favorite crossing site pretty beat up. Once the elk knock down a section of fence they use that crossing every day unless they are spooked. If there are deer using the same fields, they will take the low spot in the fence that the elk created and use it as their crossing, as well. Some ranchers will leave a gate or two open so that the elk will use the gate openings instead of breaking down the fence (this depends on where their cattle are at the time). A couple of years ago I got permission to hunt on a ranch that hadn't been hunted in twenty years. The ranch foreman told me that there were about ninety to a hundred head of elk using an alfalfa field every night. When I asked if he knew where they were bedding, he not only told me where, but mentioned that he had purposely left a gate open so that the elk would go through the gate instead of wrecking his fences. I immediately took off for the area he described and found the open gate easily. The elk trail going through the gate opening was dug down about four inches into the ground, AND THERE, RIGHT NEXT TO THE GATE, WAS A PINE TREE! I DON'T KNOW ABOUT YOU, BUT I BELIEVE IN SANTA CLAUS!! Because of wind direction, the stand would only work in the morning, when the elk were returning from the meadow to their bedding area. I put up my stand about twelve yards from the gate and was in it about forty-five minutes before daylight the next morning. For over an hour I could hear bulls bugling their brains out just over the hill from my stand. About 7:30 a.m. the lead cow came meandering through the sagebrush. When they all came into sight, there were ninety-one elk, and eleven of them were bulls! To make a long story short, there was a dandy 6x6 and a monster 6x6. I allowed all the cows, calves, and nine smaller bulls to go by my stand. Soon the number-two bull walked by and I drew on him and let him go. Then the monster turned, walked about eighty yards up the fence line, and jumped over just as slick as sour owl droppings! "A bull in the hand is worth two in the bush."

In the fall of 1987 I spent most of the elk rut bugling and cow chirping for a movie crew in order to make an instructional elk calling video. I bugled-in bulls for two of my hunting buddies, Gene Wensel and Roger Sandiland. Both took their bulls at twelve yards. I bugled and chirped in over twenty bulls for the film crew, but didn't find a bull I wanted. By the time I had a chance to hunt

The "Wense" scores again on a Hawg! Gene found a draw that was a natural funnel and took this buck at 40 yards the first evening he used the stand!

95

I took this bull at a fence crossing where the elk herd had broken the fence down, in October of '87. A funnel that was Elk-made instead of Man-made.

just for myself, the rut was tapering down pretty quickly. The bulls were still bugling, but getting a mature bull to come in was dang near impossible. I found a ranch that hadn't been hunted and it had about one-hundred and fifty head of elk in a big hay meadow every night. I scouted the meadow fence line about noon, and found a place where the fence was just about on the ground at one crossing and only a couple of feet high at a crossing about forty yards away. I set up my tree stand in a quaking aspen tree about twenty yards from the most heavily used crossing. About two hours before dark I came back and climbed into the stand. The wind was PERFECT. I hadn't been in the tree stand fifteen minutes before I picked out the first group of elk with my binoculars as they left the timber on the mountain side above the meadow. Soon I could see more small bunches of elk as they filtered out of the trees. Faint bugling floated in the still evening air. Elk began funneling in from a large area to the two fence crossings. Soon I could hear an older bull screaming above me and coming closer. I nocked an arrow, and got ready, in case he was a keeper. Sure enough, he was a fine, heavy bull. He was so busy chasing cows around that he didn't come right for the low spot in the fence at first, and my knees began to do the "purple honkies shake." Finally he turned for one of the crossings and headed for it at a fast walk. Since he chose the one furthest from me and was moving fast, I made a cow chirp knowing he would stop and look for the source. When the bull stopped and looked my way, I was already drawing my seventy-five pound Schafer recurve. The arrow sliced in between the sixth and seventh ribs, and angled forward through the lungs — damn, those steaks taste good!

All of us who hunt together have taken "beau coup" whitetails at fence and gate funnels! Check it out — you won't be sorry!

"Arms" or Points: I don't know of any better name

for these, although it isn't very descriptive. What I'm talking about here might be a break in a large section of timber or brush — a place where there may be an opening in an otherwise secure travel area. (If I'm still not explaining it properly, check the illustrations using the aerial photo that I have included.) Anyway, let's say there is an opening that deer have to cross to get from one patch of cover to another. Generally, the old timers will cross that opening at its narrowest spot. If a point or "arm" of timber sticks out into the opening and if there is a corresponding point on the other side, this is where the more experienced deer will cross. THEY WANT TO BE IN THE OPEN AS LITTLE AS POSSIBLE. In most cases, does and younger deer will cross there, too, but you will notice less experienced deer crossing just about anywhere.

Another point location, on which I concentrate heavily, is at the edge of feed areas. I have found over many years of scouting that the older bucks prefer entering alfalfa fields, oat patches, corn fields, or other feed areas from either low spots or points of timber that stick out into the field. They do this for two reasons: a point will offer them a chance to survey all or most of the field while still being hidden from view, and a low spot will allow them to enter a feed area without being visible to any predators.

A good thing to file away in the hair-covered computer and drag it up on screen whenever you're out there scouting is the point-to-point funnel. Whenever a buck has to move from one security area to another, he will choose the narrowest spot in an opening.

Benches: Ahhh, I just love them benches! I've taken some nice critters from tree stands because of benches, and they seem to funnel game no matter where you find them. I feel confident that I can hunt a part of the country where I've never been before, find a bench, and kill a deer from a tree stand. I hardly ever find a bench without a trail along the rim or a trail somewhere close to the base of the bench.

Usually I'll find that bucks will travel the rim of a bench, if it is timbered and/or bushy. They have secure traveling and can visually check whatever is below them. If the bench rim is open, for example a hay meadow, they will be forced to travel under the rim of the bench to avoid being out in the open (assuming that the base of the bench is timbered). I've got one spot I call Wally's neck, where there are three terrain features that create the ultimate funnel. A bench runs east to west and it is open on the rim. Sixty yards north of the bench and parallel to it is a lake. The lake shore and the bench pinch together into a dam. Talk about a triple whammy! The bucks won't walk the rim, can't go through the lake, and HAVE to cross the dam. In the last eight years I have taken eleven bucks

"Wally's Neck", with bench visible above these deer and pond behind my stand, I passed up this 5x5 of about 135 inches waiting for a bigger buck that never did show up. Hunt along those benches!

from that funnel. Each year, I change the position of the tree stand slightly.

I can't remember a bench which qualified as a funnel that didn't have a good scrape line along it either. Since all the deer are FORCED to use a funnel, it's a sure bet that bucks will watch it and mark it for doe travel. I have also found this type of funnel area to be excellent for morning and evening rattling. It is quite logical really. If the deer have to travel there, there is a pretty strong likelihood that a couple of bucks are going to run into each other there and "get into it." Keep this in mind, when the rut starts next fall, and I think you'll be pleased with the results.

The list of funnels above is only partial at best. These are the funnels that I have encountered in my hunting which is done *mostly* in Montana. If you have not already discovered the many funnels in nature, you should start looking for them the very next time you are out scouting. If you live in an area where there is snow on the ground, I would recommend that you scout your favorite hunting areas in December and January. Those tracks in the snow can tell you an awful lot that might not be anywhere near as visible before snowfall.

Some funnels are much more obvious or visible than others. Even if none of the funnels that I have described are in your area (HIGHLY unlikely), there are always some kinds of funnels. That is another good reason to use winter scouting. The snow may help you find the funnel that isn't so obvious to the human eye. If you live in an area where there is no snow at all, I'd recommend looking for tracks in areas where there is sandy soil or mud. One trick I have used in early fall if I see a suspected funnel and want to see if I've been correct in my suspicions, is sweeping an area clean of tracks and then checking it on a regular basis. I'll just take a pine bough or dead branch and gently sweep leaves and/or dirt. I rough it up enough so that tracks will be visible. Don't leave the branch lying around with human scent on it, and make sure to wear rubber bottom boots when walking to the area.

I can't overemphasize the importance of the funnel. For a beginning tree stand hunter, it is, WITHOUT QUESTION, one of the best hunting techniques of all. A less experienced hunter might have problems hunting scrapes, he might not be successful with bedding area ambushes, etc. The beginner, however, should have very little trouble figuring out funnels and determining prevailing wind, cover, and terrain. It just isn't that difficult! It's also just as great a technique for the guy who has been tree stand hunting for thirty years.

CHAPTER SIX
Creating the "Funnel"

Probably one of the most exciting things that has ever happened to me in hunting was learning how to CREATE my own funnels. Ain't no way I was smart enough to figure this one out on my own — I wish I had, though. It's a neat trick. Gene Wensel taught me this one, and he learned it from brother Barry. As Gene explained it to me, Barry was out scouting one evening and was watching a field that was heavily used by a number of deer, including three or four real "bun kicker" bucks. Apparently Barry had *watched* the behavior about to be described below quite a few times, but this night he was finally going to SEE it and register it in the hair-covered computer. (Actually, Barry's ain't hair-covered, but you get the drift anyway!)

The deer that Barry were scouting were coming from a bedding area on a ridge down to an alfalfa field. Barry noticed that does, fawns, and small bucks were hitting the fence line and going under it any number of places. Whitetails prefer going *under* a fence if the bottom strand of wire is high enough. The big-racked bucks, because of their antlers, will jump over. Being essentially lazy animals, they will look for a lower spot in the wire so they don't have to high jump to get over. As Barry watched that evening, he noticed three different large-racked bucks reach the fence line and walk down it one way, then turn and walk it the other direction looking for quite awhile, before finding a suitable spot to jump over. Alarm bells were going off inside his head, according to Gene.

The next day during his lunch break, Barry went into the meadow and did a little experimenting with the fence (WITH THE RANCHER'S PERMISSION). He took heavy baling twine and tied the top strand of barbed wire to the one below it. This created a "V" or low spot. He then took another piece of the heavy baling twine and tied it to the fence post (about eight inches higher than the top strand of wire) on the left side of the "V" and ran it to the fence post to the left of that one. He ran this twine out about six posts. He then repeated the same process on the right side of the "V." When he was finished he had a section of fence that looked much higher than normal and in the middle of it was a section that looked very low. At this point, Barry decided to leave the field alone for two or three days and see what would occur.

Hunting buddy Matt Riley selects a tree after creating a funnel on a fence. Note the string on both sides of the "V", to make the fence look higher around the funnel.

Three days after tying the fence into a "V," Barry went back to do his evening scouting from a hay barn that was down wind of the feeding area. As Gene tells it, about thirty deer came in to feed that evening. Over half of the does and fawns jumped at the "V." ALL OF THE BUCKS WALKED OUT OF THE TIMBER AND, *WITH NO HESITATION*, WALKED DIRECTLY TO THE "V" AND JUMPED THE FENCE! Barry had CREATED the funnel!

Well, you know this story got me hotter than a two dollar pistol! The next day I was in my favorite alfalfa meadow with a ball of baling twine in my sweaty little hand. I decided to go a little further with the experiment, however. I put the "V" at a location where there was a perfect tree in a down wind situation for a twenty yard shot at the funnel. I made my funnel, and took the time and trouble to set up a tree stand. The season wasn't open yet, but I wanted to duplicate the same activity as if it were about to be used. Three days later I came back at midday and found a BEATEN TRAIL leading to the funnel! There were plenty of deer AND elk tracks going in both directions. My knees were knocking! This was an AWESOME discovery!

A word of advice and caution is necessary, before I go into all of the various forms of man-made funnels. NEVER mess with the fences of any farmer or rancher without first telling them what you'd like to do and getting their permission. I did my first experimenting with the man-made funnel on my own place and watched the funnel to make sure that my cattle were not able to get over the low spot. So far I have never had a rancher tell me he'd rather I didn't tie his fences down — we're only talking about a three or four inch drop in the top wire, although visually it appears to be more. I am always careful to explain what I want to do, why I want to do it, and to make sure they know I will put everything back as I found it when I'm through hunting. Usually, the reaction I get from landowners is one of amusement — they just shake their heads and write me off as another one of those crazy guys with the weird weapon.

Since Barry discovered the man-made funnel, we have all used them with tremendous success. We have even used them in places where there weren't any fields, meadows, or concentration of feed. They even work well on high mountain "drift" fences for elk and mule deer. I hunt one area back in the mountains where we usually set up an elk camp each fall. About a half mile from the camp there is a BLM (we call this government agency the Bureau of Land MISmanagement) drift fence that they built at a cost of about $400,000. It really doesn't do anything or go anywhere, but they had this appropriation to spend. . . . You're a taxpayer. I'm sure you can figure this one out! Anyway, back to the point at hand — we found that the man-made funnel worked like gang busters even way up in the mountains. I found a spring that the elk were using for a wallow and for drinking, and experimented with the fence in an ideal spot for a tree stand. The elk had been crossing the fence just about anywhere along a quarter of a mile stretch. I set up a good funnel and tightened the fence in several places that they had loosened it. I checked the funnel again in about two weeks and found well used trails along the fence on both sides leading right to my funnel. The tracks indicated that both mule deer and elk were heavy users of the funnel.

In the fall of 1987, the elk got into one of our hay stacks before we put elk-proof panels around it. Normally, the elk would not come in to the haystacks until snow fell (late November or early December, where we live). We don't put our panels up until mid-November in most years. That

106

fall the elk hit the haystack before we had a chance to panel it. Once they taste that alfalfa hay, there is no stopping them. We immediately paneled the stack but the elk just knocked the rails down every night. My wife, Karen, decided to take advantage of the situation and try to take her first elk with her bow. There was a gate fairly close to the haystack and right next to it was a good-sized ponderosa pine tree. She set up a tree stand and purposely left the gate open. She and I then repaired the fence all around the area where the elk had knocked it down or loosened it. Then we tied baling twine above the top strand of wire for about thirty posts on each side of the gate and left the area alone for several days.

Karen checked the gate and found the gate opening was just torn up with elk and deer tracks. She decided the time was ripe! Her first evening in the stand was plenty exciting. About fifteen whitetails came in through the gate to get at the hay. Three of them were bucks, but nothing she wanted. Shortly after the deer came in, a small herd of elk came out of the timber and trotted over to the gate, spooking the deer as they did. Out of twenty-three head, there were no bulls. Karen had to wait until pitch dark to be able to climb down and sneak away without spooking the elk. The following evening found Karen back in the tree stand over her woman-made funnel. After about twenty minutes, five does and ten fawns came in. She noticed them all look up at the timber shortly after they got into the haystack. (HINT: watch a feeding deer if you want to know when some other animal is moving in the area — they will see them long before you do, normally.) Soon the deer twitched their tails and went back to feeding: a sure sign that whatever had their attention wasn't dangerous. Karen slid her bow out of the bowholder and got ready, expecting elk to come into view at any moment. Soon a real HAWG of a whitetail buck appeared and sauntered right for the gate opening. As he

Gene Wensel congratulates Karen Brunner on her 1987 Buck. He dressed at 226 lbs. and was taken in a created "funnel" — an open gate.

went through the gate, Karen drew her Schafer recurve and center punched him right where the lungs are supposed to be. The buck scalded out into the meadow. About eighty yards off, he cut a hard left turn and went end-over-end. He had six points to the side, and he field dressed at 226 pounds. The arrow was right to the nock and would have gone completely through him if it hadn't broken the off-side shoulder and lodged there — a great argument for the old reliable Zwickey broadhead!

Karen gave the tree stand a rest for a couple of days before going back into it. Each day we would have to go down to the meadow and put the rails back up on the panels around the stack. What had been a nice, neat haystack was a mess and reeked of elk urine. Three nights after she killed her big buck, Karen was back in the same stand. Again, about fifteen deer showed up and began to feed. Just before the end of legal shooting light, the elk came out of the timber just as before and headed for the gate. This time there were about forty head and there were two spike bulls with the herd. NONE OF THE ELK EVEN WALKED THE FENCE LINE LOOKING FOR A PLACE TO CROSS — THEY JUST "BEELINED" FOR THE GATE!

Karen chose the spike with the tallest antlers, and came to full draw as he came through the gate. She released when he was in the same spot where her buck had been when she had shot him. The bull didn't even know he was hit! At the sound of the bow string, the elk jumped and trotted off about fifty yards and just stood looking at the haystack and gate area. No sign of a hit, but Karen knew that the arrow had hit home, although she felt it could have been a paunch shot. Karen gently scraped her bow against the tree bark and the elk got just nervous enough to wander into the timber along the river. With shaking knees, she climbed down and headed for the pickup and home. After we discussed the shot over supper, we decided that, if it were a paunch shot, it would be far better to wait 'til morning than chance trailing with a flashlight and jumping the bull if he were still alive.

When we woke up the next morning there were at least two inches of fresh snow on the ground and no blood trail! We got a couple of friends and started gridding the area where the elk had gone when Karen left her tree. On the chance that the bull had been paunched, I sent one guy into some real thick brush that was near the route the elk should have taken. It wasn't ten minutes before he let out a whistle to indicate that he had found something. He had literally walked over the dead bull which was, indeed, paunched. Karen had her first bull elk with bow and arrow. She was getting positively deadly with that Schafer recurve, enough so that I started calling her "Sir"!

The man-made funnel will work in a great number of

Karen with her Spike Bull taken from the same gate opening as her Buck. He was recovered the next morning — covered with fresh snow! "Gridding" the area turned him up when there was no blood trail.

situations and in virtually any area. In 1986, I was invited by an old family friend to hunt in New Hampshire for whitetails. My interests really lay with trying a few western tricks on eastern whitetails in eastern terrain, rather than shooting anything. It was a neat experience to hunt in the hardwood forests and find old cellar holes and stone walls, where it looked like virgin forest. While hunting along an old stone wall one day, I noticed a fair number of deer tracks coming up to the wall and paralleling it. The tracks were mostly headed the same direction I was, so I followed them along. Pretty soon I found where a section of the stone wall was fallen down and all the deer tracks crossed there. There were also tracks coming from in front of me and funneling in to the crossing.

I spent about two hours (and blew any chances I had of seeing any deer) moving stones from another spot in the wall to the place where it was broken down. When I was done, the low spot had been repaired and there was a new funnel about forty feet away. A couple of days later, after several inches of new snow had fallen, I went back and, sure enough, all the tracks were funneling through the newly created low spot in the wall. You could also see where the deer had walked to the original crossing out of habit, had seen that it was no more, and had then walked further on to the new crossing.

Another trick that I tried in the 1987 season was blocking a regular trail with a fallen tree. I did this in a spot where there had been a trail for years that was just about thirty yards too far from any good tree stand site. There was a huge larch tree that was dead and would make good firewood, so I felled it to block the trail, so that the deer would have to walk around it. Within a couple of days the deer were walking around the top end of the huge larch, which put them much closer to my tree stand site.

111

This fir tree fell over in a wind storm. Mule deer and whitetail are feeding together on needles and spagnum moss. Hint: Hunt where trees have fallen naturally or where logging is going on — in cold weather the deer love this high carbo and protein feed!

There was an unexpected bonus with this set up: the deer stopped in the top branches of the old Giant and fed on the spagnum moss that was tangled in the limbs. As luck would have it, no real "hawgs" came by that tree stand, but I could have easily taken fifteen or twenty deer there!

I want to stress again the need to use your head when working with "created" or "man-made" funnels. DON'T DO *ANYTHING* THAT WILL JEOPARDIZE YOUR RE-LATIONSHIP WITH THE PRIVATE LANDOWNER! It's HIS land. He paid for it, works to keep it up, and he pays the taxes on it. He doesn't owe you "didley squat"! You are hunting there as his guest, and it's up to you to maintain the image of the hunter as a responsible person, who respects his land and his rights. I haven't ever been turned down in my requests to build funnels, because I go out of my way to be courteous and explain what I want to do, and why. (Gene calls me the "Silver-Tongued Devil"! He says I could talk an Eskimo out of his mukluks!)

As I have said several times in this book, I scout year-round. I find December scouting the most productive for the reasons I have already mentioned. I also do a lot of photographing when I'm out there. It's not only fun, but it helps me record what I've seen and some of the experiments I have tried. You will see a number of photos in this chapter that were taken in December of '86 and '87 of deer traveling through man-made funnels. I found that I could combine scouting with learning more about creating funnels, while photographing deer reactions to the funnels. It turned out to be a tremendous learning experience for me, and I would recommend it highly. For one thing, it's a whole lot smarter to "play" with man-made funnels during the off season than to do it when you are seriously trying to "stick" a big buck.

Virtually any animal can be made to travel through a "created" funnel. All it takes is a knowledge of your quarry and the area he inhabits. It will work for bears,

A created funnel at a gate approaching a hay stack. This funnel was created after the hunting season for photographic purposes plus some scouting.

wild hogs, elk, mule deer, javelina ... heck, it MIGHT even work on wild turkeys. It's one of the most exciting hunting tools there is, and its potential is almost unlimited.

I know that some guys are gonna start screaming that creating a funnel is not a "fair-chase" hunting practice. I know that I'll get letters about not "playing fair" and taking advantage of game animals. Someone out there will find fault, for sure, and claim that all the big bucks we have taken have been taken illegally or unfairly. There is so much jealousy in the world of hunting (especially bowhunting) that it is beyond belief. I'll say this. There is NOTHING unfair or illegal about outsmarting your prey by attempting to change or modify his route of travel! The ONLY thing that you have that is superior to his protective senses is your BRAIN — the hair-covered computer. If you can take him in his "living room" and defeat his eyes, ears, and nose, you have OUTSMARTED him — you HAVE NOT CHEATED! So, to any of you chronic "bitchers" who find fault with creating a funnel, let me say this in advance: "BUZZ OFF, BOZO!"

We've covered the "Created Funnel" in pretty good detail. I and my hunting partners have only used it for a couple of years and are still learning and experimenting with it. Next time you're out there scouting, look around you and see where you can "create" a funnel. You can create one at any time of the year. It's better to create one six months before hunting season than the day before hunting season. The deer will be more familiar with it. Go for it — you'll be amazed at the results!

CHAPTER SEVEN

Match the Normal

Years ago I hunted a place known as the "Peterson Ranch." Old Bill Peterson, the owner, was an old-time Montana cowboy and one of the friendliest old guys you could meet. He was lean and weathered looking with a "cowboy tan" — the kind where there is a dark, leathery look to the face and neck. If the cowboy removed his shirt and hat, though, you'd see a sharp "v" of tan caused by his open collar and a razor sharp line of tan to "ghost-white" just above his eyebrows where that hat had been every day of his life.

We'd stop by to get permission and pick Bill's mind as to what big bucks he'd seen and where. Bill would always stop what he was doing, roll a cigarette (one-handed, of course) and fill us in on the bucks he was seeing. From the stories, this old boy should have been a bowhunter! Every time we talked to him when he had been down in his river-bottom hay meadows, he would tell of the the big bucks he had seen at fifteen or twenty or thirty yards! We'd go down and still-hunt these deer, and almost never get within bow range. (All this was happening back in the days before I had been taught to SEE instead of watch.)

Now this may sound like some kind of a "yarn," but you'll just have to take my word for it — IT AIN'T! One year during the Christmas holidays, I sat bolt upright in bed one morning about three o'clock (that's A.M.) with this crazy idea that I had been missing something and had to talk to Bill Peterson. (It may have been just average brilliance, or it could have been all the onions in the salad that I had eaten for dinner. Considering my usual performance, it was probably the onions!) I called Bill about ten in the morning and asked him what he had been doing all the different times he had seen all these big bucks just standing around or lying in their beds at such close range. I could tell by his voice that he was certain that I had finally gone off the deep end or was paddling somewhere with only one oar in the water. After some coaxing, Bill told me what he assumed was obvious — he had seen all these bucks at close range while driving his tractor!

. . . Riding his tractor! The alarm bells were going off, as if an air raid were in progress! After four years of being hammered over the head with the obvious, it finally hit me. This old boy had been driving his tractor through those meadows for thirty or so years and NEVER ONCE HAD HE MOLESTED OR DISTURBED A DEER FROM THAT TRACTOR! Now it all came together. If I wanted to take one of those big bucks, all I had to do was get on the back of Bill's tractor with bow in hand, and plug one as he stood watching the tractor go by. RELAX. I wouldn't do that, nor would you. THAT isn't fair chase! What was important here was the idea of routine happenings. The deer were tuned-in to the fact that if Bill drove through there on his tractor there was nothing about which to be concerned. I later found out that he got the same results driving his pickup, although when he bought a new one, it took about a month for the deer to become relaxed with the new color and sound!

Although this lesson didn't help me to take a big buck on Bill Peterson's ranch, it was a tremendous help for me in scouting and, much more important, in installing tree stands in areas very close to the deer I was hunting. I think the best thing I can do for you, the reader, is tell a story about a buck I was hunting in this general time frame. Once I describe the buck, his behavior, and how I finally took him, the point of this chapter, MATCH THE NORMAL, will be solidly driven home.

THE STORY OF "OLD GLASSY EYES" — I knew of and hunted "Old Glassy Eyes" for three years before I ever saw him. He didn't have a name (other than "that big S.O.B.") until I saw him — then he became "Old Glassy Eyes." I had two complete sets of his shed horns and a horn from one side only for one year. From the looks of his sheds, he probably scored close to 170 in at least one or two different years. His rack was very wide and low. It was obvious that it came out straight from the sides of his head, rather than going up several inches before swinging out to the sides.

One of "Old Glassy Eyes" racks put together from sheds. The guy who did it for me didn't get it anywhere near wide enough — would have scored about 176.

117

I was scouting a river-bottom ranch that I hunt a lot, when I first found the HUGE tracks in the moist dirt along the river bank. From the depth of the tracks I could tell he was very heavy compared to other deer that were walking the same trail. His tracks were not only extremely large, but the hooves splayed out with large dewclaw marks easily discernable. This guy was a HAWG! I tried to figure him out all that hunting season with no luck at all — he was *totally* nocturnal! I never saw the buck with his rack on. In late December, I picked up his sheds near a stack yard. (For my eastern readers, a stack yard is an area that a rancher has fenced and will have several haystacks in it. The rancher feeds stock in the area around the stack yard.)

The following two seasons went the same way; I never saw the buck with antlers on and never saw a buck without antlers around the stack yard with an extra large body that I thought might have been the big one. I did, however, pick up his sheds — both of them one year, and

The first time I saw "Old Glassy Eyes" I knew he was the buck for which I had hunted so long. Note how flat he held his ears.

only one the next. Finally, in early April, when I was out scouting and taking pictures from one of the haystacks, a monstrous buck showed up in the late afternoon with a group of a dozen bucks. I knew I had never seen this buck before. His body was immense compared to the other bucks, and I could see immediately that he was VERY old. He was deeper from shoulders-to-brisket than any deer I had ever seen. His hip bones stuck out, and I could see he was stiffened up by his walk. His windpipe hung slack in his hide. His walk, though stiff and arthritic, was so majestic and "all-man" that it was clear that he was the dominant buck in the area. The attitudes of the other bucks bore this out; all he had to do was move a certain way, and they gave him room.

The buck's most striking features were his ears and eyes. There could be no doubt that this was the buck I was after — HIS EARS WERE HELD PERFECTLY HORIZONTAL FROM HIS HEAD! He had carried that flat, wide rack for so many years that his ears were permanently horizontal. When he got in close to the haystack, I got a good look at his eyes. They were milky-gray, as if he had cataracts. It was then that I began calling him "Old Glassy Eyes".

As the green grass came up, all the bucks began to fill out and lose their winter hair. The older bucks started growing new antlers, and the bases of the antlers on "Old Glassy Eyes" were huge. With only a couple of inches of growth, they were already growing out to the side. About this time, "Old Glassy Eyes" went nocturnal, and subsequent scouting trips gave me no sign of him other than tracks on the river-bottom trails.

In early August I was heading down to fish the river that ran through the ranch where "Old Glassy Eyes" lived, and decided to get there before daylight so I could glass the alfalfa fields right at dawn. I left my rig at the

"Old Glassy Eyes" in the stack yard growing his last rack. Note the hanging windpipe and massive old body. New antler growth already indicates heavy bases and a flat wide rack on the way.

stack yard and got into an old permanent tree stand from which I could glass the entire meadow area. As dark turned to misty gray, I could make out the movement of several deer drifting toward the river bottom bedding area. Their path of travel would bring them within sixty or seventy yards of me. As they moved closer, I could see the outline of a HUGE rack on the lead buck. They were grazing along as they came closer, and by the time they reached my stand, I could see them well. "Old Glassy Eyes" had a rack I guessed to be around twenty-four inches wide. He had seven points on one side, one of which was a four inch "dropper," and nine points on the other! This old boy was a real "BUNN KICKER"! I knew I had to take him!

I hunted him all of the archery season, which lasts for five weeks in Montana. There was no rut activity, and I hunted him on approaches to hay meadows and approaches to bedding areas. I never got so much as a look at him — he was "nocturnal" as usual. The evening before the last day of archery season found me sitting in a new tree stand location. I was playing a long shot and not hunting the main alfalfa fields, where most of the deer activity was. I was hunting a little patch of alfalfa back in the timber where I had previosuly found little sign. (Any one with any BRAINS would have hunted there instead of the other, more populated meadows. I think we have already established the fact that I am a slow learner, however!) There was a little point of timber that stuck out into the meadow opposite my stand. Beyond it was a brushy ridge that I would SEE today as the only logical bedding area to serve the field. Back then, I thought the bedding area was the river bottom where all the does and younger bucks were bedding. Just before dark, I spotted movement in the timbered point across from my stand. Shortly after I saw the movement, four large racked bucks grazed slowly out into the alfalfa. One of them was my huge quarry — with his nine point antler broken off a couple of inches beyond his brow tine! The three bucks that were with him were all in the "one-hundred and thirty to one-hundred and forty-five inch" class. "Old Glassy Eyes" wouldn't "score," but that didn't matter. I had finally seen him, and if I did everything right, he COULD be mine!

I waited 'til a half hour after full dark and climbed down out of that tree stand as quietly as I could. I SLITHERED out of there, making sure I didn't give the bucks so much as a clue to my presence. My mind churned all the way home. For the VERY FIRST TIME, SINCE I BEGAN HUNTING, I RELIED COMPLETELY ON THE HAIR-COVERED COMPUTER. Gene had been coaching me on this buck, and I had been learning on my own, as well. As

I was driving along, pondering the situation, a whole bunch of thoughts began to come together.

Rob King of Illinois took this 154⅜ buck over a scrape line. He wrote, "Your stand is great, deathly quiet, the most comfortable stand I've ever hunted out of, and it's so easy to put up."

I knew that my only chance to take this buck lay in ambushing him in the little point of timber,from which he had entered the alfalfa patch. I was equally certain that I couldn't walk into that patch of timber and put up a tree stand without ruining the whole set up. The bedding area was only about two-hundred yards from the ambush site. The buck would hear (and probably see) any activity that took place there. THIS IS WHEN MY CONVERSATION WITH BILL PETERSON, ABOUT HIS SEEING BUCKS FROM THE TRACTOR, HIT ME. I KNEW HOW IT COULD BE DONE! As soon as I walked in the door of my house I got on the phone to the rancher, explained my plan, and got his approval for what I wanted to do.

At noon the next day, my wife and I showed up at the ranch house and borrowed the rancher's truck and a hammer. We then drove HIS TRUCK down the ranch roads into the hay meadow. I pulled up next to the fence that surrounded the field, and Karen and I got out. I banged the tailgate open, and Karen and I talked in normal voices as we went about carrying out my plan. Karen took the hammer and began tapping the staples that held the barbed wire in place on the fence posts. As she did that, I quickly screwed in my tree steps and installed my tree stand in the tree that I figured best covered the route the bucks would use coming into the field. When I was finished hanging my stand, Karen and I "twanged" the fence a couple of times, slammed the tailgate, and made "leaving" noises. I quickly changed into hunting clothes, grabbed my bow, and got in the stand. As I did this, Karen drove slowly down the fence line as if she were checking the fence from the truck. Soon she was out of sight, heading back toward the ranch buildings.

I sat in the tree stand thinking. I had at least five to six hours to wait before any buck in his right mind would come out to feed. Thoughts raced through my mind. Had I done the right thing? Had I blown it on the last day of archery season? Was matching the rancher's NORMAL BEHAVIOR going to fool the deer? I had bet everything on a learning experience, from another location and another situation, hoping that it would work here. One thing began to develop as I sat there thinking for five hours . . . CONFIDENCE! I was CONFIDENT that I had made the right play by the time evening feeding hours arrived. That CONFIDENCE is one of the most important ingredients in the perfect bowhunter stew!

Just before the end of legal shooting hours, I saw movement about seventy yards away in the brush along the field. One, two, three shapes moved out of the brush, jumped the fence, and began to graze in the alfalfa. It was the three bucks that had been with "Old Glassy Eyes" the

252 lbs. and 12½ years old — "Old Glassy Eyes" was a true Monarch. My most treasured trophy, for a lot of reasons.

previous evening! No sign of "Old Glassy Eyes." I waited. It was getting darker and darker. Some guys will tell you it's hawg-wash that you can sense a presence near you. I'm here to tell you, it's not! I FELT THAT BIG OLD BUCK COMING!! I turned my head ever so carefully, KNOWING that he was coming from behind me. Out of the corner of my eye I saw him, walking that incredible "monarch" walk. As he came out of the gloom to walk by my stand at twelve yards, his eyes were on the bucks that were already feeding in the meadow. The seventy-five pound Robertson Longbow came up smoothly. As my fingers hit anchor, I released and the compressed cedar arrow angled in between the ribs and sliced on through the old monarch. He "crow-hopped" a couple of times, then walked out into the meadow and looked around. His head began to drop, and with considerable effort, he walked into a patch of tall grass in the edge of the meadow and collapsed! HE WAS MINE!

What you have just read isn't some made-up yarn — it's a true story of SEEING and THINKING! It's a demonstration of the fact that you CAN outsmart a whitetail. You can beat him at his own game! There are many ways to out-think a whitetail (or any other critter, for that matter), but one of the best ways to take a big old buck is to do your scouting and hunting in a manner that matches, *as much as possible*, normal activity in the area in which your quarry lives.

THINK about some of these following ideas. If you are scouting in farming or ranching country, match your travel METHODS and TIMES to those that are carried on by the landowner in his NORMAL routine. When hunting new property, I'll ask the rancher where his ranch roads are and GET PERMISSION to drive them. I'll find out if he walks or rides a horse, four wheeler, or pickup truck. I'll find out WHEN he might NORMALLY be in the area I'd

Gene with a nice buck taken when he matched normal ranch travel patterns. The rancher dropped him off at his stand and then went on to cut firewood. Gene took the buck ten minutes after getting in his tree stand.

like to scout. By MATCHING HIS NORMAL BEHAV-
IOR as much as I possibly can, I am far less likely to
disturb the deer! If you go walking through an area where
no one NORMALLY travels on foot, you are going to
alarm the deer. O.K., so deer get alarmed quite often — so
what's the big problem? The problem is that the walk you
took (scouting or whatever) will alert a SMART OLD
ANIMAL to the fact that something out of the ordinary
has occurred AND WILL VERY LIKELY CAUSE HIM
TO CHANGE HIS BEHAVIOR AND/OR MOVEMENT
PATTERNS!

You can easily rationalize about matching normal
activity in an area and say to yourself that this is only of
importance either just before or during hunting season.
So what if you spook the deer while scouting three months
before the season? By hunting season, they'll be back to
their standard routines, right? Yes, that is right.... But —

126

you are probably going to see a lot more of what is there in the way of deer if you can pass that scouting trip off as normal farm travel. We NEVER saw some of the big bucks that Bill Peterson described, when telling us what he had seen from the seat of his tractor.

One thing you can count on, I *NEVER* carry a tree stand to its "hang-up" spot on foot, unless there is no other way. Now, this rule may not hold true for the area in which you hunt, but in Montana, there is no such thing as a walking cowboy! I can't remember seeing a rancher walking around his ranch. They either use a pickup, a four wheeler, or a horse. I can usually get a pickup within fifty yards of where I want the stand. I'M NOT LAZY! I *LIKE* TO WALK! I drive to the stand location because the deer will pay very little attention to the truck or four wheeler.

I set up one extremely productive stand last year

Gene took this buck from a stand that was so close to its bedding area that there was no good approach on foot. He had a rancher drop him at his stand while he was on his way to feed cows with a pickup truck!

awfully close to a really super bedding area. The stand HAD to be in that spot, there was no alternative. I knew I couldn't walk to it without blowing out a couple of dandy bucks, which would probably cause them to change their bedding area. I mentioned it to the rancher, and he said he'd been meaning to knock down and cut up a dead tree right near the spot for firewood. When I volunteered to go with him and help him split wood, he was delighted, and I had a way to get in there and set up. We spent about three hours cutting, splitting, and loading firewood right next to my preferred stand location. My stand went up, and I was in it an hour before daylight the following morning. I saw four bucks from that tree stand that morning. Unfortunately, the one-hundred and forty incher that walked close enough to hit had one antler broken off from fighting.

When I am entering a tree stand, I'll consider matching normal routines, too. If a pickup truck would normally drive close to a tree stand location in mid-afternoon, I'll try to get someone to drop me off at the stand site. I figured this out quite simply. Several times in the past I have carefully STALKED my tree stand and climbed in only to have a rancher drive by just about the time I hoped the deer would begin moving. The first few times it happened, I climbed down in disgust 'and gave up. At some point, I stayed in the stand and found that the deer movement hadn't been affected by the NORMAL passage of the ranch vehicle.

There are going to be a lot of times, however, when you can't approach your stand in such a manner. When you are in a situation where an approach on foot is necessary, always remember to STALK your stand. Approach it with the same caution you would use when making a stalk on a deer. If your stand location is a good one, there could be a buck there already.

CHAPTER EIGHT

Scents and Nonsense

This is bound to be a touchy subject, since the scent industry is one of the fastest growing archery related businesses today. Let me point out a couple of facts before we get into the scent thing:

1. I DON'T MANUFACTURE SCENT!
2. NO INDIVIDUAL OR COMPANY IS PAYING ME TO PROMOTE THEIR PRODUCT IN THIS BOOK!
3. I HAVE NO PERSONAL GRUDGES, OR "AXES TO GRIND" AGAINST ANYONE IN THE SCENT INDUSTRY.

I put scents into two categories: negative scents and positive scents. To me, the negative scent is the most critical for the hunter. NEGATIVE SCENTS ARE THOSE SCENTS THAT YOU CARRY INTO THE WOODS WITH YOU THAT IDENTIFY YOU AS MAN! There are so many negative scents that it would be impossible to list them all, but a partial list of the most common ones will give you a good feel for what we are talking about:

1. Cooking odors
2. Cigarette smoke
3. Any kind of perfume, or perfumed soap, shampoo, toilet paper, etc.
4. Gasoline
5. Breath
6. PIT ODOR!
7. Any number of household odors

8. Chemical odors

These are just some of the most common problem scents that the unsuspecting or unthinking hunter can carry into the woods with him. Most bowhunters are more aware of human scents than rifle hunters would be, because of their need to get so close to their quarry. There are a few bowhunters out there, usually newcomers to the sport, who are totally unaware of negative scents. There are a whole lot of bowhunters who ARE aware of negative scents in general, but UNTHINKINGLY carry one or more of them into the field with them.

I've talked to bowhunters who are extremely aware of keeping themselves and their clothing clean, but then make that one little mistake that can ruin their chance for that trophy animal. Drive out before daylight during bow season and check out the U-PUMP-YER-OWN gas stations. Without fail, you'll see some guy in camo pumping his own gas. He just isn't thinking or he forgot to fill up the day before and hoped the gas smell wouldn't get on his clothes . . . NO CHANCE!

Ethel's Greasy Spoon Cafe — every town has one. You know the place: they haven't changed the fat in the deep fat fryer for five years (they just add more when the level gets too low). Try to get THAT smell out of your wool hunting clothes! It's tuff enuff getting it off your skin and hair. Invariably, some hunter will stop in at Ethel's for breakfast or to pick up a candy bar, not realizing he is polluting himself.

I've never been able to understand a hunter who claims to be serious about his sport at the same time he is reaching into his shirt pocket for a cancer stick. We won't even talk about the fact that you're gonna die if you smoke. As my Daddy used to say, "If you're gonna be stupid, ya gotta be tough!" Cigarette smoke STINKS!

*When we're hunting areas with multiple deer tags, we take every spike we see. Studies indicate spikes are genetically inferior in areas with high protein feed. Matt Riley did the honors here, and he is **super** careful about negative scents!*

There ain't a critter out there that isn't gonna pick you off from three-hundred yards away. I've even had guys give me that lame excuse, "Yeah, well I smoke in the woods so I can watch the smoke and tell the wind direction." Gimme a break! The STINK stays in your clothes and your hair, and your breath stinks like the bottom of a very dirty ash tray. If you are really serious about killing big critters with a bow, don't smoke, don't go where there is smoke, and don't hunt with a smoker or drive to the hunting spot in a smoker's vehicle.

Perfumes of any kind should be public enemy number two (second only to tobacco smoke). Everything in our world is perfumed now. The great marketing and industrial complex has determined that they need to ruin the American public's sense of smell and supply them with constant butt rash! Just walk into your local super market. You can find the soap and detergent section easily WITHOUT READING THE AISLE SIGNS! Just follow your poor over-worked nose. Talk to any skin doctor and he'll tell you that allergic reactions to perfumed products have sky-rocketed in the last fifteen or twenty years. Think about the hunter in the average household. His wife does the laundry in "New Blue Cheer." I don't know about the blue part, but the soap smells like a Parisian whorehouse . . . pardon the expression, but it does! Then he uses scented *"DEODORANT"* bar soap in the shower. As soon as he's done with that he reaches for the SHAMPOO. Check the last three letters of the word . . . POO . . . I rest my case! Now he zips into the kitchen for coffee and, you guessed it: bacon . . . oh no!! He cooks the bacon in his hunting clothes AFTER the shower. Then all that breakfast brings on the normal call of nature, and guess what he uses to clean that up. You got it: PERFUMED TOILET PAPER. (He also rolls some of this stuff up and puts it unthinkingly in his pocket for use in the woods in case of emergency.)

Scented feminine "deodorants" and perfumed tampons are a real no-no for lady hunters. Check the labels on those products, before you buy them.

Gene Wensel is one of the most careful people I know when it comes to avoiding negative scents. See the results?

EVERYTHING seems to be perfumed now-a-days. It takes real work on the part of the hunter to avoid this stuff. Since the average guy doesn't do the shopping and/or washing, it makes it even harder for him to get away from the perfume syndrome. I am very fortunate on two counts in this problem area: my wife HATES perfumed household products to begin with, AND she's a hunter and understands the need to avoid this stuff at any cost. Later in this chapter, I'll list some of the products we have discovered over the years that are not perfumed.

Armpits. Walk along in any public place and you get this incredibly bad odor of sour armpits. How come everybody around the offender is swooning but the guy or gal with the pit odor can't smell a thing? I'll wonder about that one 'til I'm ninety. I know one thing: I can sure smell MY pits when they get rank. (The WORST offenders, by the way, are the waiters who serve you the thirty-dollar dinner . . . after they reach across you to put your plate down, your appetite is gone!) I know a lot of bowhunters who take care of themselves in the keeping clean department, and their pits stink. Gene Wensel got a free sample of a fabulous product called "Pit-Stop." This stuff is made from two flowers that grow in Egypt and Israel. Two thousand years ago, ancient healers used the paste from these flowers to keep wounds from becoming infected. It seems that these flowers, when combined and ground into a paste, become a powerful anti-bacterial agent. You shower at night just before bed, put the "Pit-Stop" on your pits, crotch, and feet. Take a shower immediately after you wake up the next morning and wash with an unscented, non-deodorant soap like Scent-a-Way or Ivory . . . NO BODY ODOR! That's right, NO BODY ODOR! AND, IT LASTS FOR TEN TO TWENTY DAYS WITHOUT ANOTHER APPLICATION! Gene tried "Pit-Stop" when he was in Michigan in August on a trip. He wore the same "T" shirt for four days in ninety-degree weather, and then had his wife and kids do the sniff test. There wasn't a whiff of pit odor!

Household odors are really tough to fight. Even if you keep away from the worst of the perfumed products, you can't avoid the normal run-of-the-mill smells that go with living in a house. Most hardcore hunters will have their washable clothes done in unscented laundry soap (if you can find any), and they'll have their wools drycleaned. After this, they'll store them outdoors or in a grain bag filled with leaves and pine needles. This definitely helps a lot. It's extra work and a hassle, but it is one of the steps you can take to get rid of as much negative scent as you can.

Breath. The human mouth has a strong odor. No matter what you do, it is going to have SOME KIND OF A SMELL TO IT. I got the answer to this problem from PLAYBOY MAGAZINE, believe it or not. Some dude wrote in to the PLAYBOY ADVISOR column and asked what to do about morning breath when he wanted to kiss his sweetiepie awake. PLAYBOY replied by recommending that he keep a basket of fresh apples by the bed. Now I have whatever breakfast I'm going to have (BEFORE I shower, etc.), brush my teeth and gargle, and then I eat a nice fresh apple. It does help! According to the old timers, it keeps the doctor away, too! Chewing gum and breath mints are out! I have no idea whether it really works or not, but I NEVER breathe through my mouth, if I can help it, while on stand.

Chemical smells of any kind are really bad. I can't make a list of them here because, there are so many, so you will have to think about the chemical smells that you might be likely to encounter and figure out a way to avoid them. Some might seem insignificant, or even silly, but you need to consider them. I rode in a guy's pickup early one morning to go elk hunting. I could smell something really strong, when I climbed into the truck, but couldn't place the odor. As we rode along I asked him what I smelled. It seems his teenage son had cleaned the truck the day before and used an upholstery cleaner on the naugahyde seats. I had to get my wool pants and shirt cleaned the next day.

Another REALLY bad one is SNO-SEAL shoe grease. I apologize for hammering a particular brand, but this stuff is a real disaster for bowhunters and rifle hunters alike. It's so full of chemicals that it smells like some science lab, and I'm here to tell you that it doesn't waterproof your boots and eventually eats the stitching out of them. We use a natural product called "Montana Pitch Blend." It was discovered by a guide years ago when he got fed up with the smelly stuff mentioned above. It is a combination of pine pitch, beeswax, and mink oil. The stuff is a terrific waterproofer and leather conditioner, AND it smells like pine pitch. It can actually be used as a cover scent.

Use the hair-covered computer and really go through all the things around you in your daily life that could be negative scents. At this point in time, there is no known way for a human to have no smell at all. I'm not going to give you a magic formula that will make deer walk right up to you from your down wind side. That just ain't gonna happen. What you TRY to do is MINIMIZE your human scent impact, and then cover it as much as possible.

We've talked about negative scents. Let's talk about positive scents. This will also bring up the subject of NONSENSE! You can define a positive scent as any scent that will help cover your human scent, any scent that will attract game as a food scent, or any scent that will attract game as a sex scent. They can also interact. An apple scent might act as both a cover scent and as an attracter scent, etc.

The problem for the hunter in determining what kind of scent to use and what brand to use can be referred to as the NONSENSE. There are DOZENS of scent companies out there selling TENS-OF-THOUSANDS OF GALLONS of scent, and the vast majority of it is not what it is claimed to be! Consider this — there is one major scent manufacturer who puts out a ton of pretty tasteless and slick-o advertising for "DOE-IN-RUT, BUCK LURE." Rumor has it that at one major sports show, this company sold over *three-and-one-half million dollars* worth of this so-called doe-in-heat estrus scent. I asked one of the most respected wildlife biologists in America, John Craighead, how many deer this guy would have to have to collect this much *estrus* urine. John thought about it and came up with this answer: the scent company would have to have about FIVE-HUNDRED THOU-SAND whitetail does in captivity. Each one would have to have an external thermometer attached to it to help determine when it came in heat. Urine would have to be collected at that precise time, in order to be truly "estrus." You decide — do you think there are that many captive whitetail deer anywhere? Check the advertisements — they don't say, "whitetail doe *deer* estrus urine," they say, "whitetail doe in estrus urine"! (Ever notice that domestic rabbits have whitetails and are called does if they are females?)

I asked both John Craighead and Gene Wensel how a company like this could get testimonials about how well their "doe-in-estrus urine" worked. Both gave me the same answer: A buck in the rut will react to almost any urine smell. Since rabbits come in heat so often, there is bound to be so-called "estrus" smell to a fair portion of the urine, which would also help attract bucks. Those of you who have read Gene's first book on HUNTING RUT-TING WHITETAILS will remember that Gene freely admits to hanging used tampons near tree stand locations as an attracter — AND THEY DO WORK!

It's really sad that bowhunters are set upon by unscrupulous scent manufacturers. A hunter puts in all the time and effort of locating hunting spots, obtaining hunting permission, scouting, putting up stands, and then runs the risk of spooking deer by using phony scents. The uninformed hunter assumes that, because one or two companies really pump out the advertising, they must have a good product. He or she doesn't realize that the BIG companies are the ones most likely to be passing off phony scent. It is the small companies, limited in growth, because they have a few deer and only use real deer urine, who are the most likely to have the "real thing".

Some time ago, Gene Wensel was writing an article for BOWHUNTER MAGAZINE on scent. Gene was able to obtain information from only one scent manufacturer, James Valley Scent Company. It seems they had real deer and were using bladder bags to collect urine. We know for certain that three other companies have real deer, as well. They are Hunter's Specialities, Buck Stop, and Robbins Scents. I'm sure that there are other companies that have deer, too. Even with the companies that really have deer, the standard collective procedure is allowing the deer to urinate on a sloping cement floor. The urine is bound to mix with feces, dirt, and any other pollutant that is on the floor. The only way to get guaranteed deer-estrus urine is to collect it in a bladder bag from a doe that is temperature checked to determine when she is actually in heat.

If you are going to use liquid scents, ask around and try to determine which companies have sound reputations for good products and honesty in dealing with their buyers. I would recommend buying from small companies. There is ABSOLUTELY NO WAY that any company that sells large volumes of liquid scent can own enough deer to produce those volumes, especially if they are calling it *estrus* scent! Be especially aware of the companies with many pages of high pressure "slick-o" advertising in the major magazines. These are the outfits that are most likely to be cheating the hunter.

I have had very mixed results with doe deer in estrus scents. I have used scents, both liquid and wafer, that I was certain were the "real thing" in a lot of rut situations. Sometimes they bring the deer right in, and sometimes deer will walk right by them and pay no attention whatsoever. I think a lot of it has to do with weather, the percentage of does in heat in the area at the time, and the buck-to-doe ratio. I can generally count on the fact that the scent may work for a day or two, and then the deer may totally ignore it for a couple of days.

A couple of years ago, I was hired by the Hunter's Specialties Company to develop elk calling diaphragms for them. One of my hunting partners and I designed and field tested a line of diaphragm calls and a "grunt" tube

A food scent wafer gets crunched by a black bear. This one happens to be a bacon wafer.

for them. In mid-fall that year, they sent us some new experimental scent "wafers" to try out. I have to admit that my first reaction was, "Oh brother, another gimmick!" We were filming whitetail hunting, when I put the first "Doe-Deer-in-Estrus" wafer in a scrape and set up our tree stands for shooting and filming. When we left the stands after dark that evening, I forgot to remove the scent wafer from the scrape. The next morning we returned before daylight and took our stands. There had been a "skiff" of snow that night. When it was light enough to see, I could see a set of dragging tracks going to the scrape and out of it. We had no action that morning; I climbed down and went to retrieve the scent wafer, but it was gone! The buck tracks led up to the scrape, and then I could see where the buck had rubbed his muzzle in the snow, where the wafer had been. The only possible explanation was that he had picked the wafer up in his mouth and taken it away! I immediately called the president of Hunter's Specialties,

*A nice whitetail that has come in to an estrous scent wafer. This one is made from **real** doe deer-in-heat urine — not the phony stuff!*

Dave Forbes, and asked him if he thought such a thing were possible, or if I was "nuts." Dave told me that I was the forteenth "field tester" who had either witnessed or experienced a buck carrying off a scent wafer.

So far, I have had only positive or neutral results with the Doe-Deer-in-Estrus wafers. Either the deer are strongly interested or pay little attention. I haven't had any negative results, such as a deer spooking at the wafers. I personally believe the wafers work, but I'm not at all that excited about using a "sex attracter" scent, because the deer seem to be so "on and off" about them. In the fall of 1987 in Montana, I never witnessed one buck come in to either wafers or liquid estrus scent, even though I hunted every day for thirty days straight. I talked to one of my hunting partners whose brother and some other hunters used the sex wafers in New Jersey during the same time period. He said that they had bucks come to the wafers every day, and one morning his brother had eight bucks come in!

I really believe there are a lot of different factors that affect the use of sex scents. As I mentioned above, in the 1987 rut, the sex scents just didn't work at all in Montana. In the 1987 rut, we were in the worst drought in recorded history, and none of the game animals were following normal behavior patterns that entire fall. Also, our buck-to-doe ratio was the healthiest it has been in twenty years. On top of that, there was a high percentage of mature bucks from four-and-one-half to seven-and-one-half years old. The hunters in New Jersey were dealing with different weather conditions, different buck-to-doe ratios, and a MUCH DIFFERENT age mix on the bucks. I am convinced that the older, more experienced bucks are less likely to react to a sex scent than those young bucks. If I figure out the answers to the sex scent question sometime during the next fifty years, I'll reckon that I'm lucky!

I just received a new scent wafer a couple of weeks ago that I'll be testing in the 1988 rut. This is one about which I'm pretty excited. It's called "Buck Intruder," and is made from the hock glands of whitetail bucks. The idea is to put out the smell of a rutting buck in order to bring the area's dominant buck in to run the intruder out. For years, we have used fresh hock glands cut from bucks we have killed as a lure and cover scent.

I'm much more interested in cover scents than I am in sex scents. For me, as I said above, the sex scents are "on again, off again," and totally dependent on the rut and a lot of other factors. The cover scents, however, WHEN PROPERLY USED, can be a real help to the hunter at any time of year. KEEP THIS IN MIND: assuming you have

I photographed this buck after the season in a deer yard. The wind was blowing in every direction. Pine cover scent wafers kept the deer from winding me. This buck is going to get hunted hard in the fall of '88!

done your scouting, and assuming you are SEEING instead of watching, and you store all the stuff you have SEEN in the hair-covered computer, the cover scents are far more important than the sex scents anyway. Why? Because with all homework done properly, you are going to know where that big buck lives, where his scrapes are, where he is bedding, and where the doe concentrations are. You have a much better chance of ambushing him along a known travel route than you do of luring him in to a sex scent. Therefore, your main concern should be getting rid of all the negative scents that you can, and COVERING all those left over.

There are several important things to remember about cover scents:

1. NO COVER SCENT IS FOOLPROOF! You will NEVER get rid of, or cover, all human odor, no matter how efficient you are in removing and avoiding negative scents. At best, you are covering as much human scent as possible and then using all your other knowledge to keep the remaining human scent away from your quarry.

2. You must use the correct cover scent for your area. Using sage cover scent where there is no sagebrush ain't gonna cut it. If I'm in an area where there are lots of pines, I use a pine scent wafer. If I'm hunting elk in an area where the sagebrush comes up into the timber, I use a sage wafer. Sage and pine are both good STRONG cover scents, and they are NATURAL. You walk through a patch of sagebrush and you SMELL SAGE! For years I rubbed crushed sage leaves on my shirt and pants when I was out in the field. Now I use the wafers. They are easier to use, stronger, and re-useable.

3. When you can't buy a cover scent, use the ones in nature. A good green cow flop is about the best there is and seems to work almost anywhere. When I'm out hunting I'll try to keep fresh cow manure on my boots all

143

day; it helps a lot.

4. In cold weather liquid cover scents don't seem to work anywhere near as well as they do when it's warm. So far, in the testing I've done, the scent wafers seem to work no matter what the temperature. I suspect that liquid scents might wash away, or be diluted in heavy rain. This won't happen with the wafers.

It's hard to believe that a man with a face like this could pour skunk scent in the men's room in a major airport . . . isn't it? Hmmmm!

A word about skunk scent. When do you smell strong skunk odor? You smell strong skunk odor when a skunk has been ALARMED! If you stop and think about that, you will probably come to the same conclusion we have. Skunk stink is likely to put the deer on alert for whatever predator caused the skunk to spray. Gene Wensel used the stuff during a long layover we had in Chicago when we were traveling together one time. He poured a bottle of the stuff in one of the stalls in the men's room, and we spent three hilarious hours sitting across from the entrance watching the reactions of passengers, janitors, and airport officials. I wanna tell you, it SPOOKED a whole lot of "critters."

Scents are critical to the hunter. You have to do everything in your power to keep yourself and your clothing neutral, and then cover all remaining human odor that you can. As long as you're ONE-HUNDRED PERCENT CERTAIN that the sex scent you are using is not fake, then use it — DURING THE RUT, NOT BEFORE! It may work or it may not, but try it and see. It's just one more tool that may help get the job done. Use cover scents wisely and don't become so reliant on them that you become careless about wind and travel patterns.

CHAPTER NINE

Clothing and Equipment

I consider clothing and hunting equipment to be one of the most critical factors in successful tree stand hunting. You may have done five or six months of careful scouting, found and patterned a really dandy buck, and put up your tree stand in the perfect spot. If you aren't using proper clothing and equipment, you could blow the whole effort in a few seconds.

Clothing is one of the most important factors in ALL types of hunting, although the majority of hunters don't realize it. Clothing offered to bowhunters is one of my pet peeves. Just look in the average outdoor catalog or sporting goods store: most of the "camo" clothing is made of fifty/fifty cotton and rip stop nylon. THIS STUFF IS THE NOISIEST CLOTHING IN THE WORLD! This is the stuff our military people wear. Put them in the jungle in another war, and their CLOTHING is going to get them killed!

YOU MUST WEAR TOTALLY QUIET CLOTHING! When you have a deer or an elk twelve yards from your tree stand, he will hear the sound of your shirt sleeve moving when you draw your bow, unless the shirt and all your clothing items are QUIET. I bought a real top quality set of wool "camo" clothes a few years ago. The designer had the right idea, but he wasn't a hardcore hunter and hadn't had enough hunting experience to really understand what was needed for the PERFECT garment. He made a heavy, top quality wool hunting shirt, and then lined the inside of the collar with nylon. I didn't pay any attention to the collar liner, probably because I was so excited about the first wool "camo." I put the shirt on over my heavy polyproplyene long underwear and set up for a big buck on which I was working. The buck came in at about fourteen yards. When I drew my bow, my whiskers scraped on the nylon collar lining. Needless to say, the buck jumped the arrow by a country mile, and never came by that scrape line again.

As far as clothing material goes, there are four basic materials that are quiet: wool, Polar Fleece, moleskin, and one-hundred percent cotton. (As of this writing, there is a new cotton/poly mix that is SUPPOSED to be as quiet as one-hundred percent cotton. If you find a garment you like in this stuff, check it out carefully before you buy it.)

We use both light and heavy cotton clothing early in the season, when it is likely to be anywhere from sixty to ninety degrees. That's just too hot for wool. When we get a new set of cotton clothing, we wash 'em several times in unscented soap such as "Scent-A-Way." It takes five or six washings to get rid of the stiffness of cotton. Even after repeated washings, cotton still has some noise factor when walking through brush. When we're stalking we use UNLINED wool gaiters. Woolrich Company manufactures wool gaiters. Because their clothing designers weren't hunters, the gaiters are lined with waterproof nylon: end of silence factor!

Several years ago we designed a long-sleeved "camo" T-shirt with a binocular pouch in the front. We use this as a long underwear top. When the day warms up, we take off our outer shirt and stow it in fanny pack or day pack. The "Bino" shirt solves the problem of binoculars thumping your brisket while you are moving, and keeps the "binos" out of the way if you have to take a shot. We now make them in a light-weight cotton tiger stripe, and a heavier fabric called "Interlock," which comes in a TreBark pattern.

As the weather begins to get colder, we generally switch to light wool and/or moleskin. L. L. Bean puts out a really nice pair of light green moleskin pants. They are high quality and match the color of sagebrush, cottonwood trees, and quaking aspen trees very well. I usually buy charcoal fabric paint and paint some "squiggly" vertical lines on them for a "camo" effect. Just about every catalog and sporting goods store will offer charcoal gray wool pants in light and heavy material. Charcoal gray is a darn good color for tree stand hunting. Now we are beginning to be able to get good wool pants and shirts in "camo" patterns. King of the Mountain offers the heaviest and best quality wool clothing I've seen in "camo" (tiger stripes: one of my all-time favorites). Tree Bark™ "camo" is now available in wool. Mossy Oak™ is a new "camo" pattern and one of the most impressive I've seen. They have a full line of one-hundred percent cotton clothing, and are just about to come out with some first-class wool and Polar Fleece clothing.

No one seems to make a LIGHT wool "camo" shirt at this time. There is a time period in the fall when you want to wear wool shirts, but you want one that's lightweight. Most people wear some sort of long sleeve shirt under the wool shirt, because wool usually makes you itch if worn next to the skin. We have solved this problem by hitting the local "western" clothing stores. They generally offer a large selection of lightweight, *checkered* wool "cowboy" shirts. If you get the right color, the checker pattern is as good as most "camo" patterns, especially if you are up in a tree.

As the weather gets colder, the new Polar Fleece garments come into use. They are now offered in a variety of "camo" patterns, and are light in weight, extremely quiet, and incredibly warm. We even found them to be very impressive as windbreakers. We generally wear these just over standard-weight long underwear or over light cotton clothing, which we wear over standard weight long underwear.

Once temperatures drop down into the range of twenty degrees or colder, we get pretty serious about keeping warm. The best time to take a trophy buck is during the rut, and in MOST hunting areas the temperatures are getting right down there during that time period. The colder it gets, the better I reckon my chances are to take a really big buck or two. In REALLY cold weather the deer move constantly (especially if spurred on by the rut), and there are few other hunters out there. If you can figure out

Here's a "Keeper". I took this photo three days after the season ended. But, he'll be bigger next year and I know I'll get him then . . . .

150

a way to stay in a tree stand for three or four hours when it's fifteen below zero, you have a super good chance to take a "hawg."

It's really difficult to find QUIET clothing that will keep you comfortably warm WITHOUT BULKING YOU UP SO MUCH THAT YOU CAN'T SHOOT YOUR BOW ACCURATELY. Our small group of hunting partners probably have one-hundred and fifty years of combined hunting experience. It has taken all of that experience coupled with new developments in fabrics and clothing design to get us to the point where we can be warm in almost any kind of weather: warm enough to stay on stand for the hours needed to take trophy bucks. We have

147 inches of proof that the guy who dresses for extreme cold brings home the bucks. It was 27 below zero when the Author "stuffed" this buck. (He wasn't wearing the clothes shown in the photo.)

had to search in unusual places to find specialty items. We've spent thousands of dollars on clothing that wasn't as advertised. We've even had to design and make our own clothing items: now that's hardcore desperation!

The space program and the military have made our search for warm and quiet clothing much easier. New fabrics, like Polar Fleece, polyproplylene, and others have really helped to wick away moisture and provide warmth. The military has developed ECWCS (Extreme Cold Weather Clothing Systems) clothing. Through the Freedom of Information Act, it is possible to find out about these garments, although extremely difficult for the average guy to get his hands on them. When it's really cold, we try to "layer" up with some of these specialty items. They provide far more warmth than clothes used five years ago, while allowing excellent freedom of movement: exactly what the combat soldier in artic conditions needs. Hmmm — this is exactly what the bowhunter needs, too. Very coincidentally coincidental!

For our first layer, we use polypropylene long underwear tops and bottoms. But they aren't NORMAL "polypro" material. They are MUCH thicker and were designed for the Armed Forces. They are called "Extreme Cold Weather Polypropylene Thick Survival Underwear." The top has a zippered turtleneck. Zipped up, it keeps the neck and chin very warm. Unzipped, it allows heat to escape if the wearer is walking. This stuff alone is terrific with just good wool clothes over it. When you use the next "goodie" with it, you can stay up in the tree for hours at twenty below zero: it's called "ECWCS Fiber Pile." Again, this is a military item. It consists of a fiber pile shirt and low-top bib overalls, and is designed to go over the above mentioned long underwear and under your outer layer of wool or Polar Fleece. When you use this combination of under layer, middle layer, and outer layer of good heavy wool — YOU'RE WARM. You have complete freedom of movement, and your clothing is totally silent. With proper care, an outfit like this will last for fifteen or twenty years.

The only clothing items we haven't discussed are boots, hats, and gloves. During the early weeks of archery season, when it's likely to be quite warm, I wear the old reliable L.L. Bean boots with the leather tops and rubber bottoms. I have a high pair with fourteen-inch tops and a low pair with six-inch tops. Although there are now a lot of imitations, I have never seen a better quality pair of boots, and L.L. Bean stands behind their products one-hundred percent! We dress the leather tops with Pitch Blend leather dressing to preserve the leather and stitching and give them a pine scent. (Beware of the copies made in Taiwan — Boy, are they JUNK!) The rubber bottoms are really important for the tree stand hunter because they won't hold and leave odors. When I'm wearing my "Bean" boots, I generally wear a medium-weight sock of wool, or wool blend. A medium pile sock helps keep your feet from "fatigue" when standing or walking.

For head gear I usually prefer a "camo" bandanna worn as a head band. I really dislike hats in warm weather, because they really pick up odors from sweaty hair. With the head band, I cover my advancing forehead (notice I didn't say receding hair line!), and if it's hot, the head band keeps sweat out of my eyes.

If I wear any gloves at all, I use a light cotton "camo" glove made by Hunter's Specialties Company that has a special weave that makes the glove grip the bow handle better. Even though our quarry seldom look up, I think it's a good idea to wear a camo glove, especially if you are wearing a ring. One flash of sunlight off that ring, or even a white knuckle, could cost you a trophy.

For mid-fall when it's beginning to get colder, but isn't

At -15° you can keep warm and quiet if you dress right. Hunter pictured here is wearing ECWCS with wool over it, Bunny Boots, Balaclava Helmet, and "Woolie Booger"™ mitts! You still have freedom of movement by "layering" your clothes.

yet unbearable, I go to an insulated rubber boot or a shoe pack. I've had great luck with a pair of Red Ball, all-rubber, insulated boots over the years. I hadn't seen any in my local stores for a long time, but just found out that they are still on the market with even better insulating materials than they had ten years ago when I bought this pair. In my mind, when a boot is labeled "insulated," it means it MIGHT keep your foot warm at forty degrees, IF you wear the right socks. My old Red Balls — I better re-phrase that one! — My old Red Ball Boots seem to do pretty well down to twenty degrees. After that, I go to "Boot Packs" (use the ones with heaviest felt liners).

At this time of year I go to some kind of a knit wool hat — my preference is a "camo" Balaclava Helmet. I can wear it as a hat or pull it down to cover my face as it gets colder. For gloves at this time of year I use the lined version of the Hunter's Specialties gloves mentioned above. I cut the first three fingers off of the right hand of the gloves to accommodate my shooting glove.

When it's really cold, you gotta get hardcore! At twenty below zero or colder, the hands and feet will let you down every time! If any part of you starts to get cold, it starts a chain reaction, and you're DEAD MEAT! For years we suffered because of hands and feet giving out when the deer were moving all day due to extreme cold. The military uses two different boots that were designed for the Korean War: the "Mickey Mouse" boot, and the "Bunny" boot. The "Mickey Mouse" boot has a couple of layers of felt MOLDED INTO THE RUBBER BETWEEN THE GROUND AND THE USER'S FOOT. It also has an air pocket between the inside and the outside, and is supposed to be good to twenty below zero. I had a pair of these boots, and I won't buy that claim! The "Bunny" boot is another story — this sucker REALLY WORKS! It has three layers of heavy felt molded inside the sole. Its most important feature is an AIR BLADDER that holds a lot of air (the BEST insulator), and can be blown up with a valve on the side of the boot. The boot is good to SEVENTY BELOW ZERO, and I ain't gonna find out if that claim is accurate! A word of caution — Army/Navy stores offer these boots as surplus. I went through nine pairs. They wouldn't hold air and they were worn out. Don't waste your money on used boots; buy a new pair. With a little care, they'll last you for years.

I solved the problems of cold hands in 1986. I sat in a tree stand with all the goodies mentioned in the preceding paragraphs, and it was about twenty below zero. My hands got so cold that I could only stay about a half an hour. I had to leave my stand just as it started to get light enough to shoot! I went home and took a long hot shower. When I got out of the shower, I stood on a sheep hide bath mat to dry off. It was one of those un-shorn hides that I later found are called "rugs" in the tannery trade. All of a sudden, alarm bells were going off. I went into my den

This is one of the tree stand hunter's best tools. The saw folds to fit in pocket or fanny pack and has a threaded handle so you can clear shooting lanes. When the manufacturer quit making them, I started to produce them myself.

and outlined my hand on the hide. I cut out four u-shaped pieces of hide and then stitched one piece to another to make a "bag," with the wool on the inside, that fit my hand with a little room left over. What I had was a large, deep pair of mittens with no thumbs that went up my wrists to just overlap my shirt cuffs. I ran a string from one through my belt loop on my right side, out the belt loop in the back of my wool pants, to the other mitt. By doing this, I reasoned, the left mitt would drop BEHIND me and out of the way of my bowstring, when I had to shoot. The next morning when I used them, it was again twenty below zero with a fairly stout wind blowing. I stayed in the stand for four hours and took two Pope and

Of the twenty or so tree steps made, The EZY-Climb is the best we've ever found. It is the safest and most stable, and quiet to install.

Young class bucks! I actually had to take my hands out of the mitts, because they were hot. These things were so fantastic that I patented them and now manufacture them — I call them "WOOLIE BOOGERS." Every hunter who has used them has said about the same thing: "Now I can finally hunt with WARM hands!"

For super-cold weather socks, I would recommend some of the new wool blends that have a very thick "pile" on the inside. I use "pile" socks when stalking elk, but I opt for a "medium pile." Even though they are a little too warm, the pile is a much better cushion than a plain cotton sock and you're much less likely to be plagued with blisters. I just go with thicker socks as the cold weather progresses.

There is one other clothing item that we have used and recommend highly. The Filson company makes some really good quality wool clothes, and several years ago we found a couple of their wool vests in a Western clothing store. The vests were charcoal gray with darker charcoal checkers. We reckoned that they would be great torso warmers and wouldn't impede arm movement at all. We were delighted with them and have been using them now for about eight years. They are darn good wind breakers, and have side pockets for keeping hands warm.

Equipment

Before we get into the discussion of equipment, I'm going to make a statement that you should remember when you read my opinions on the subject. I may criticize some of your equipment, BUT I AM *NOT* CRITICIZING YOU! Please be open-minded, when you read my opinions. They are just that . . . opinions. They are, however, opinions based on thirty-one years of bowhunting experience of my own, and over one-hundred years of combined experience of my hunting buddies. I have owned and shot compound bows, longbows, and recurves. I have used almost every different type of broadhead there is in hunting situations and in test situations. I have tried very hard to view innovations in archery with an open mind, in order to better determine which ones were useful hunting tools and which ones were useless and unnecessary junk. All I ask is that you be open-minded, and willing to change your ideas, if I can show you a better way. I have no reason to want you to do it "my way." My concern is that all bowhunters use the most efficient equipment to achieve their goal of taking the life of a game animal in a quick and humane manner.

This section ought to get some of you bowhunters stirred up, because it deals with equipment. Seems every time equipment comes up, somebody gets excited. I think it's because human nature dictates that you have to defend a product, if you have already purchased it. Usually when a person has purchased something, he has done so because it was SOLD to him. To admit that it may not have been a good purchase is to acknowledge that the buyer got sold a bill of goods and made an unwise purchase; and noboby likes to do that! I'll be the first to admit that I've made a BUNCH of unwise purchases over the years. I hate to think of how many dollars I've blown on stuff that didn't come close to doing what it was supposed to do. I finally quit relying on the advice of slick-o salesmen and went to "reputation" stores and catalogs, or did my own research, and learned by trial and error. When I go into a sporting goods store, I ask subtle questions of the sales clerk about hunting. I can tell immediately if the guy is a real hunter of just some loud talking dude, who THINKS he knows something about hunting. If the latter is the case, I walk out and go else-where.

I personally think archery shops are the worst for this sort of thing. Because I am in the archery business, I travel a lot and go to a lot of archery shops. You wouldn't believe how little some of these "behind-the-counter-experts" know about bowhunting. Yet these are the guys who sell "Joe Newcomer" $600 worth of "ABSOLUTELY NECESSARY" bowhunting gadgets. The name of the game for these archery shops is "sell as much as possible, with as many replaceable-type items as you can," because it's a seasonal business. You can just about hear the digital cash register "beeps" in their brains, when a newcomer to the sport comes in and says he needs advice on bowhunting equipment. NOT ALL ARCHERY SHOPS AND THEIR COUNTER SALESMEN ARE LIKE THIS, HOWEVER. You have to find a shop where there are some experienced hunters, and you are far more likely to get good advice. Just remember, these guys are still likely to try to sell you more than you really need to be a successful bowhunter, because that's their business.

You will probably be surprised that I'm not going to talk about bows first. I'm going to talk about broadheads — that's the thing that kills the quarry. Regardless of the bow you use (assuming that it will propel an arrow), the broadhead and the arrow are the most important equipment items in achieving a clean kill.

BROADHEAD SHARPNESS AND PENETRATION ARE THE MOST IMPORTANT CONSIDERATIONS IN THE TAKING OF BIG GAME ANIMALS! If a broadhead is not SHARP, you have no business shooting it at any animal. A dull broadhead can cost you an animal. Even worse, a dull broadhead may cost that animal its life, in a slow and agonizing death. NEVER RELY ON FACTORY EDGES TO BE SHARP ENOUGH FOR HUNTING! Check them out and sharpen them yourself. I recently received a sample of half-a-dozen "hunting" heads from a manufacturer. They were the "razor blade insert" type of heads with four blades and a four-sided point. On the outside of the box there was a printed message that said, "Caution! xxxxxxxx makes 'em sharp!" I took one of the heads out of the box and checked one of the "razor-sharp" blades. I couldn't believe it! It was so dull I couldn't break the skin on my thumb when I ran it down the blade UNDER PRESSURE! (See photo.) How many hunters went into the woods with those heads last fall?

None of us who hunt together use replaceable blade broadheads. We have had very bad results with them, while hunting, and in some pretty reliable tests we conducted. We tested over fifty broadheads for penetration in a rather unique way. We mounted SHARP heads on aluminum shafts and placed the nock on a digital scale

*Here's a factory "pre-sharpened" blade right out of the box. My thumb was **moving** in this photo. Note the pressure I'm applying. **I could not cut my skin!** Should you hunt with this head?*

with the broadhead pointing up. A fresh steer hide was stretched in a frame and then forced down over the broadhead. When the arrowhead penetrated completely through the steer hide, the weight necessary to achieve full penetration was recorded. "Chisel point," two-bladed broadheads penetrated with less pressure than all other broadhead designs. The Zwickey Eskimo head was the best, going competely through the steer hide at just under five pounds of pressure. Heads like the Bear Razorhead™ the Hunter, and the Hill head all went through at about five to six pounds pressure. The best penetrating "replaceable blade" head went through at just over twenty-five pounds of pressure — MOST of them went through between forty and fifty pounds of pressure! The two worst heads, the Wasp and the Savora, WOULD NOT PENETRATE THE STEER HIDE AT ALL — THE ALUMINUM SHAFTS BROKE BEFORE PENETRATION COULD BE ACHIEVED!!! Both of these heads

This is a WASP head. Check out the round "bullet" point. Pushing it through a hide is like trying to push a live .30-06 cartridge through. . . . 'Nuff said?

have round, "bullet point" type points on them. Trying to push them through the steer hide was like trying to push a .30-06 bullet through the hide — ain't no way!! (See photos.)

When you are hunting from a tree stand, your choice of broadhead design is even more critical than if you were hunting on the ground. Why? Simple — when you are

"A picture is worth a thousand words." Check out my hands. I'm using all my strength to try to get the Wasp to penetrate. Instead, the arrow shaft fractured. (Try to catch THAT on film!)

shooting down at an animal you have a much higher likelihood of hitting major bone, such as the spinal column,
shoulder blade, or upper leg bone. This is especially true
as the angle of your shot gets steeper. When you are
shooting straight down, you have at least a fifty/fifty
chance of hitting the back bone. This is where penetration
becomes REALLY important. I think our test proves,
beyond a shadow of a doubt, that the "chisel point" head
is the best choice by far for hunting from tree stands AND
for hunting on the ground. Our hunting experiences bear
this out, as well. All of us have tried the "replaceable
blade" heads and, without exception, found they were
inferior to traditional heads.

Should you shoot a two-blade or multiple-blade head?
That's a choice you have to make. In our group of five
bowhunters who frequently hunt together, three of us use
two-bladed Zwickey heads, and two of us use the four-
bladed Zwickey heads (the third and fourth blades are not

*Check out my hands. I'm using only thumb and forefinger and
NO EFFORT to pull the hide down over the Zwickey Big Delta
head. It is the best penetrating Broadhead in the world!*

164

full-size — they are small "bleeder" blades). My feelings are that if you hit bone with a two-blade head, you are merely slicing through it. If you hit bone with a multiple-blade head, you are trying to SPREAD the bone in order to get through it. This is especially true of heads with five and six blades! All this bunk about needing a lot of blades to cause bleeding and leave a blood trail is just that — BUNK! It is ADVERTISING HYPE THAT IS GEARED TO MARRY YOU TO THEIR BROADHEAD. Why are you "married" to their broadhead? The answer is really simple, if you think about it. You have already spent the money on the heads. When you shoot one of these heads, you have to use replacement blades made to fit that particular head. (Once you shoot one of these heads, you can't successfully re-sharpen the blades, you have to install new ones.) Once you have purchased the UNBE-LIEVABLY EXPENSIVE replacement blades, then you are stuck with those heads forever. It is a vicious circle that has been carefully planned by the manufacturers!

I personally don't believe these multiple-blade heads cause any *significant* increase in bleeding. I do see one very critical problem with them. If they are, as we believe, poor penetrators, and if, because of that, they don't create an exit wound, where is your blood trail? With a high entrance wound, which is likely if you are shooting from a tree stand, and no exit wound, all the bleeding is very likely to be internal. If you don't hit heart or lungs you could lose an animal that may die within the hour.

Over the years I've heard bowhunters talk about wanting the arrow to stay in their quarry so that it cuts internally as he runs. I don't buy this at all. My experience has been that the "pass through" kills them FAST, leaves one heck of a blood trail, and is less likely to be felt by the animal. It zips through so fast that often the quarry will take a few jumps and stop to see what the com-

165

motion was, and fall over right there in plain sight. You achieve a pass through with a very sharp, PENETRATING broadhead.

A hit in the shoulder blade puts 'em down when you shoot heavy shafts and sharp, chisel point heads. Penetration is the name of the game!

Arrow weight never used to be a consideration for bowhunters. Arrows generally weighed from five-hundred to seven-hundred grains, including the broadhead. You shot wood, fiberglass, and later aluminum. Now-a-days, the "gadget makers" have come up with the overdraw system in their never-ending quest for more arrow speed. The idea behind the overdraw is to enable the hunter to shoot a shorter, and therefore, lighter arrow to achieve higher speeds. These arrows will weigh under five-hundred grains. In some cases there are bowhunters out there who are hunting deer and elk with three-hundred and fifty grain arrows. This is CRIMINAL! AN ARROW THAT LIGHT, *NO MATTER WHAT THE SPEED MAY BE*, IS A POOR PENETRATOR! Penetration is much more a function of weight than speed.

In his newest book, Gene Wensel talks about the same thing. I'm going to take the liberty of quoting a brief passage: "Let's say we have two white balls the same size. One is a ping pong ball, the other is a golf ball. Throw each of them as hard as you can into a snowbank. Which one is going to penetrate deeper into the snowbank? I rest my case. Velocity cannot make up for weight in penetration. Hunting arrows should be heavy, not ultra-fast. By every law/rule of ballistics, penetration is *weight* plus velocity."

Somewhere along the line, the manufacturers decided that they had to hype speed. In order to do that they had to use light arrows. Without any thought to the game that would be hunted with this equipment, they began the big "Madison Avenue" sales pitch. No matter what you see in magazine ads, no matter what your buddies shoot, just remember: NO BOWHUNTER SHOULD HUNT ANY ANIMAL WITH AN ARROW THAT WEIGHS LESS THAN 550 GRAINS, INCLUDING THE HEAD! A six-hundred and fifty grain arrow seems to be the ideal in terms of penetration, speed, and flight performance. If

167

some dude in a sporting goods store tries to tell you this ain't so, pay no attention to him — he's either ignorant, trying to sell you lots of add-ons, or BOTH. If he sneers, asks you who filled your mind full of nonsense, and then says that Paul Brunner don't know nuthin' when you tell him you read it in my book, PUNCH HIM IN THE MOUTH AND GO TO ANOTHER STORE! (Tell him it was from me, the "World's Shortest Bowhunter.")

Bows — a tough subject. You can shoot any darn bow you want. You will note, however, that most of the "old-time" bowhunters who have consistently taken trophy animals year after year, are shooting recurves or longbows. I'll share my thoughts on that with you, and let you decide which is best for you.

There are plenty of good hunters out there who shoot the compound bow. I don't care what they use for a bow, as long as they are RESPONSIBLE bowhunters. Most of the compound shooters, whom I have known, generally make the switch to recurve or longbow once they discover that they really love bowhunting. Why? Simplicity for one thing. A recurve or longbow will weigh less than two pounds. It is nothing but a "stick" and a string. Generally, the "stick" is handcrafted out of beautiful wood, which makes it aesthetically pleasing to carry in the woods.

The old myth that the "stick" bow is slow and inefficient is just that — a myth. The average compound will shoot a hunting weight shaft at 189.6 feet per second. I do not own a longbow or recurve that shoots under 190 feet per second! I own two custom Schafer recurves that consistently chronograph over 220 feet per second! (Read my lips: OVER 220 FPS!) Most bowhunters will find that the "stick" bow is much better for snap-shooting. By that, I mean it is much faster to swing up, hit your anchor, and accurately release an arrow. When the compound lets off, or "flops over" it breaks concentration and destroys (momentarily) the shooter's fluidity.

The "stick" bow is much less hassle for the shooter. Most guys I know who shoot compounds are constantly fiddling, adjusting, and tuning. I just slap an arrow on the string and let her fly! There's no such thing as "tuning" a "stick" bow.

Again, let me say that I am NOT opposed to the compound bow. I have owned them and taken game with them. I just enjoy the beauty and simplicity of the "stick" bow. I also find that I shoot far better with it at game. It is easy to shoot instinctively. I compare it to shooting with a finely balanced custom shotgun, or fishing with a fine bamboo fly rod. The "stick" bow becomes a part of you: an extension of your body. I doubt that anyone can truthfully say that of a physically heavy compound, especially when it's equipped with four or five pounds of add-ons.

As a RESPONSIBLE bowhunter, I am very much concerned with the proliferation of gadgetry that has come about BECAUSE of the compound. In other words, I don't feel that the compound is the villian in the sport of bowhunting. The villains are the gadgets that the "mad-cap" inventors and manufacturers have introduced to accompany the compound. Very few of these inventions are really necessary to make the bowhunter a GOOD bowhunter! After all, we are supposed to sharpen our SKILLS, not rely on TECHNOLOGY, to become better, MORE RESPONSIBLE bowhunters!

IF YOU LOVE BOWHUNTING, YOU HAD BETTER THINK ABOUT THIS: In virtually every state, bowhunting seasons, which are very liberal, are referred to as "primitive weapons" season. If and when WE ALLOW bowhunting to become technical, then game departments are going to tell us that our weapons are NOT primitive, and put us in with the gun hunters! NOTE: I said above, if WE ALLOW . . . . THAT'S RIGHT! IT'S UP TO US. WE HAVE TO BE THE ONES TO SAY, "NO!" We have to tell the manufacturers that enough is enough. We, as bowhunters, have to go to the game departments and say, "We don't want these gadgets used during archery season, because they are unnecessary and bad for our sport."

Let's look at some of the gadgets that have come into use with the advent of the compound:

Sight Pins: If you use them, think about this: they only work when the bow is held PERFECTLY VERTICALLY! The minute you cant your bow, they no longer work properly. Now, I don't know about you, but I rarely get a shot in the woods where I can stand up and hold my bow vertically. I generally am shooting under or around some sort of cover, or I am kneeling and HAVE to cant my bow.

Back in the days when I was still shooting (and tuning) a compound, I met a guy at a bowhunter's dinner named John Schulz. John changed my bowhunting forever. He was the last living bowyer who had been taught to bowhunt and build bows by the legendary Howard Hill. After he spoke and showed movies of Howard Hill hunting in Africa, I told him of my frustrations with the compound, and of all the game I was missing with the sighting system. He invited me to come to his shop the next day and shoot a longbow.

When I arrived at John's shop, he had me shoot a sixty-pound longbow into some hay bales for form — not for accuracy. As I shot the bow (which was as light as a feather and really FUN to shoot) he explained that was how Howard Hill taught shooting. Shoot for form until you have it down pat, then worry about where the arrow is hitting. That first afternoon, John finally had me shoot an eight-inch plywood disc out of the air. When I achieved that "miracle" I turned to John and asked how long it would take him to build me a bow. He said, "Oh, you're not through yet!" As he reached into his pocket and hauled out a silver dollar and tossed it up into the air he said, "NOW hit this!" Just as he had taught me, I swung the bow up smoothly and "center-punched" that silver dollar — that was the end of gadgetry for me forever.

Today, although I still shoot longbows and love them, I am shooting recurves a lot. I do like the recurve better for tree stand hunting because of its shorter length. I also happen to be hunting with Paul Schafer quite a lot, and it would be pretty tacky to hunt with a different bow in his company, since he makes bows. (Paul was a pro football player, and since his arms are bigger around than my thighs, it would also be stupid and dangerous to hunt with some other brand of bow!) He builds one of the most beautiful recurve bows in the world. It also happens to be the fastest, although I still don't see speed as the all-important answer.

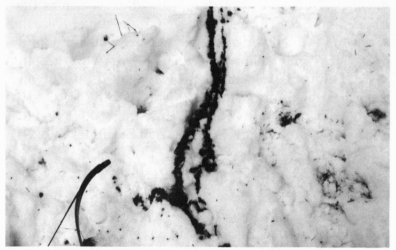

You don't need gimmicks like the string tracker if you take only good shots, use the best Broadheads, and shoot heavy shafts. That combination gives you a blood trail that a three-year-old kid could follow!

171

The String Tracker: This item was designed to make someone a bunch of money, but it don't belong on a hunter's bow! You hook the string to your arrow so that when you hit the animal, you don't have to worry about finding a blood trail, you just follow the string. The manufacturer guarantees perfect arrow flight out to twenty-five yards. What if the animal is at thirty yards? I have heard countless stories from guys who used these and the string hung up: no trophy! Hey, let's not forget, either, that a RESPONSIBLE bowhunter is SUPPOSED to learn how to track an animal that has been hit!

Lighted Sight Pins: I really HATE this one! If it's too dark to see your quarry well, you have no business staying in the tree stand and hunting! The lighted sight pin was designed for one purpose only: shooting after it's too dark to see well.

The Release: I really laugh when I see a guy with one of these things dangling on his wrist — they sure look ridiculous! Question: what happens when you miss that Boone and Crockett buck and you'd like to get a second arrow off? I'll tell you one thing for sure: you ain't gonna do it quickly, if you have to grab an arrow (while keeping the dangling release out of the way), get it nocked, and then look down and connect this silly thing to the bow string. It's just another gadget that you were SOLD but don't need. Your fingers are more reliable and a whole lot quicker!

The Range Finder: It takes away one of your most important bowhunting skills: that of learning body sizes and range by knowing your quarry and his habitat. Why not just go hunt with a rifle if you don't want to really learn your sport? Consider this scenario. A bull elk is walking toward you in the lodgepole. You put your bow down, fumble with your range finder (you're carrying it in a belt pouch), get the range of the elk, put the range finder back, pick up your bow, nock an arrow, and get ready to shoot. While all this has been going on, the elk has covered about seventeen yards, and your range reading is no longer accurate. (After spotting all the movement you were making, the elk is probably long-gone, anyway.) Another totally impractical gadget foisted off on the unknowing bowhunter! . . . It's disgusting!

Razor Blade Insert Heads: Again, if you want to be a REAL BOWHUNTER, you should pay the dues. Part of paying your dues is doing the extra work that the average rifle hunter doesn't do. You should learn to sharpen your own broadheads. You should use the most efficient head. Don't waste your money on stuff you don't need to be a good bowhunter.

Super-Duper, High Speed, Heated, Lighted, Sighted, Ultra-Hyper Deluxe Magnesium Cam Bow (with Over Draw): This is the one that looks like a piece of fancy construction equipment. It has a heated hand-warming grip, seven sight pins (one or more lighted), cable clamps to keep the cables in place, peep sight in the string, rubber gizmo to keep the peep sight lined up, twelve arrow quiver (do you really NEED twelve arrows?), bow sling, kisser button, and arrow stabilizing plunger. WEIGHT: 11.5 POUNDS! (Not counting batteries for the grip and pins!) You gotta be kidding me! This just doesn't qualify as a bow. I'll GUARANTEE that I can get four arrows off ACCURATELY for every one that a guy can shoot with this thing. If you are going to shoot "wheels," get yourself a good, reliable SIMPLE compound, and shoot the heaviest arrow you can. Shoot it instinctively and often, out there in the woods where it counts. I guarantee you'll miss less game, and enjoy it a lot more!

There is a truly great book that all hunters and conservationists should read. It is A Sand County Almanac by

Aldo Leopold. In it Aldo wrote, "Our tools for the pursuit of wildlife improve faster than we do, and sportsmanship is voluntary limitation in the use of these armaments. It is aimed to augment the role of skill, and shrink the role of gadgets in the pursuit of wild things. Too often, what is offered as an aid to self-reliance, hardihood, woodcraft, or marksmanship, becomes instead a substitute for such skill." All of us who call ourselves hunters should read, remember, and understand what Aldo Leopold wrote — OVER FORTY YEARS AGO — long before the advent of the compound bow and its associated gadgetry!!

I'm certain that some of my readers are torqued off at me for discussing equipment, especially bows, but I love my sport very much and am concerned at what has happened to it because of the gadgetry. Remember what I said at the beginning of this section, "I am not criticizing you — I am criticizing the manufacturers for making and hyping it, and I am criticizing the dealers who are selling it." All I ask of you is to keep an open mind. Got a friend with a longbow or recurve? Go shoot it — I think you might get really turned on. I know for sure that you will shoot a whole lot better and get a whole lot more out of bowhunting! Even if you prefer the compound, help us get rid of the needless technological devices that will ultimately sound the death knell for our sport.

CHAPTER TEN

Tips and Philosophies

Hunting for thirty years with a bow teaches you lots of little things that are really helpful in making you a better bowhunter. If you hunt with a group of bowhunters, who have also hunted for many years, you can exchange a lot of good ideas and tips. I have to admit that most of the tips listed below came from my hunting partners. Even though Gene and Barry have taught me to SEE instead of watch, I'm still your basic slow learner and need all the help I can get.

Gene Wensel: Get a very fluffy feather (like a marabou feather) and tie it to the upper part of your bowstring with a piece of waxed dental floss about six inches long. This "wind feather" will tell you the direction of the thermals when the human body can't detect any air movement at all.

John Schulz: If your shooting glove gets loose and starts to slip off your fingers when you shoot, go to a good sporting goods store and get some batter's resin. It is merely powdered pine pitch that baseball players use to help hold a sweaty bat. Dip your shooting fingers in the resin and then put your glove on. It will stay on perfectly.

Paul Schafer: If you want to be a really good instinctive shot with a bow, you need to carry a JUDO head in your quiver. Whenever you can shoot in the woods without spooking game, have that arrow on the string.

Shoot at all sorts of natural targets such as twigs, leaves, stumps, clods of dirt, etc. Paul shoots from fifteen yards out to ninety yards. The idea isn't to shoot game at ninety yards — it is to make the shooter very familiar with arrow trajectory. Once you can hit consistently at sixty, seventy, or even ninety yards, you will find you won't miss at thirty to forty yards. I can vouch for the truth of Paul's theory. Since Karen and I started shooting like this in the woods, our shooting has improved DRAMATI-CALLY!

Barry Wensel: Many of you have seen pictures of Barry and have noticed his hunting cap is always on sideways so the bill is over his ears instead of his eyes. Most people assume that he does this to keep the bill from hitting his bowstring when he draws to shoot. Not so! Barry says that if he wears his hat like this, and a deer

*Here's proof that constant practice **in the woods** with a Judo head pays off.*

happens to look up and see him in the stand, the deer will not be alarmed because it will think Barry is looking in another direction . . . hmmmmm?

Karen Brunner: Karen keeps one of her recurves strung up in the bedroom. Whenever she swings through there during the day, she picks the bow up and does a little exercise to keep her bow pulling muscles in shape year-round. Point the bow up at a forty-five degree angle and draw it one-quarter of the way and stop for a second while counting, "One." Draw another quarter of the way, stop, and count, "Two." Another quarter and count, "Three," and then, "Four" at full draw. Now let it down while doing the reverse. Do about five or ten repetitions, and then SWITCH ARMS. Even though you don't shoot with the opposite hand, this is necessary to build up the muscles along the top of the back evenly.

Paul Brunner: Lots of people who want to switch to the two-bladed broadhead like the Zwickey or Bear Razorhead want to know the best way to sharpen them. Here's what I do. Get either a Mill Bastard, Smooth Mill file, or a TruAngle™ Hone and file the blade at a flatter angle than that put on by the manufacturer. When you have the factory edge gone, you should have a nice long taper that is very sharp, BUT WITH A ROUGH EDGE. I prefer leaving that rough, or serrated, edge as it is. Some people prefer using a "crockstick," after the file, to get rid of the rough edge and achieve a razor-sharp shaving edge. I don't think this is the way to go, but everyone has his own idea of how to sharpen arrowheads. The rough, serrated edge will not corrode as quickly as a razor edge, will not dull as quickly on hair and bone, and tends to "rip" arteries and blood vessels, which I think causes more hemorrhaging.

Barry Wensel: The newcomer to tree stand hunting should practice shooting from some sort of elevated

177

position. Shooting down at steep angles forces the shooter to aim much lower than normal. The steeper the angle, the lower the hunter has to aim. You have to get used to that as soon as you start tree stand hunting or you will shoot right over that buck's back!

Gene Wensel: Gene always carries a hot water bottle with him into his tree stand. He uses it when nature calls, and refers to it as his "pee" bottle. He is really hardcore, and will stay in his stand for hours. He doesn't want to have to get down, walk two-hundred yards to take a leak, then get back into the stand, and risk spooking the game in the area. He says that the water-tight cap keeps any odor in, and it's the perfect answer for an obvious problem. Gene always claims he needs the "wide mouth" model, but I've seen him bathing in a creek and know that's a crock of El Toro Poo Poo!

*Karen never lets me hunt without a diaphragm anymore! I call, she shoots! If she gets any better with that Schafer bow, we are all going to start calling her, **"Sir!"***

Paul Brunner: Always carry a "diaphragm" with you when tree stand hunting. (We're talking about an elk diaphragm, here.) If you should see elk from your stand, even though the rut may be over, a cow "chirp" will usually bring them right to you. If you see a coyote, fox, or bear, use the call as a dying rabbit's squeal. You won't believe how fast they'll come to it. (Wolves and Griz go nuts over them, too.)

Gene Wensel: If possible, when rattling from tree stands, use two hunters. Place your tree stands about forty yards apart so that each hunter can rattle for the other. If a buck is coming in to either rattling or grunt calling, he will know within a gnat's whisker where the sound was coming from. He'll come in WATCHING THE GROUND around your tree and usually stop some yards away. That is where the shooter comes in to play. All the deer's concentration is on the area around the rattler or caller, and the shooter will have an excellent chance of getting a standing shot at the buck.

Gene Wensel: Sometimes Gene gets covered with burrs going to and from his tree stand. If he is in a motel, he doesn't want to sit around with burrs all over him and has come up with an excellent solution. He takes a blanket off the motel bed and lays it on the floor. He then lies down on the blanket and rolls himself up in it like a cocoon. At this point, whoever is with him grabs the edge of the blanket and pulls, unrolling Gene. All the burrs are now transferred to the motel blanket. Gene wonders why all the motels in eastern Montana have his name up there beside the names of those who pass bad checks! Tacky, tacky, tacky! (Do you think he REALLY did that?)

John Schulz: NEVER make eye contact with an animal. Many times during your hunting career you will get "caught" by an animal that gets close and "freezes" to stare at you, because it realizes that something isn't quite right. This can happen on the ground or while you are in a tree stand. No matter how much "camo" you are wearing, if you make eye contact with that animal while it is "checking you out," it will scald out of there. Either close your eyes completely or close them almost all the way and watch through your lashes.

Hopefully, these tips will help you. Some are told in fun, but most of them are really useful and took us a lot of trial and error (mostly error) to learn. When you discover some little thing that seems inconsequential, but helps your bowhunting, share it with another bowhunter so that his hunting improves. Bowhunting is the greatest sport on earth, and we all have to sharpen our skills in order to do justice to our quarries.

Let's talk about bowhunting as a sport in the past, the present, and the future. Why the past? The past history of bowhunting, and the men and women who participated in it, are very important to our sport. Those who bowhunted in North America in the late 1800's and the early-to-mid 1900's set the course and established the code of ethics for bowhunting. They were a very special breed of people — they were the "elite" of the hunting world. They sought to limit themselves and their hunting equipment in order to derive more satisfaction from their sport. People like Maurice and Will Thompson, Art Young, Saxton Pope, Howard Hill, and Fred Bear, to name a few, established the paths along which bowhunting was to travel.

Our predecessors in bowhunting saw the DIFFERENCE BETWEEN "HUNTING" AND "KILLING." They saw how little challenge and satisfaction there was in "blowing away" a mule deer or sheep at three hundred plus yards. They chose to impose restrictions and limits on themselves in the pursuit of their quarry and in the enjoyment of their sport. They were, indeed, "elite" in the very finest sense of the word. They were the "best," with the loftiest goals and the highest ideals, ever to enter the picture of "sport hunting." We owe them a tremendous debt for their work in establishing these restrictive methods of hunting and passing on to us a deep and abiding love of the "stick and the string." They provided us with a code of ethics for bowhunting that survived untarnished until the early 1970's. That code of ethics still survives, but not in the hearts and minds of ALL bowhunters.

In the early 1970's came the advent of the compound bow. With that bow, came a re-kindling of interest in bowhunting that had not been seen since Fred Bear popularized the recurve bow back in the early 1950's. With the compound bow came the "gadgets" and the media "blitz" of advertising that caused a surge of interest in bowhunting that was "frightening" to those of us who saw bowhunting as a sport for the "hardcore" few, rather than the unschooled many. The tremendous increase in popularity of bowhunting brought people into the sport who were unaware of the history of the sport. By being unaware of that history, these people learned little of the ethics, traditions, and self-imposed restrictions that had evolved over the years. The gadgets, "hyped" by the manufacturers and dealers, created the "instant bowhunter" (sometimes referred to as the "bionic bowhunter"). These gadgets made it easy for the first time shooter to hit a pie plate at twenty yards within the first few minutes of dealer coaching.

Most of the archery dealers in Montana advertise the sale of archery equipment most heavily in the ten days before the bow season opens. It is common to see first-time bowhunters coming out of the shops with the new eight-wheeled wonder bows and thirty pounds of accessories three days before bow season. You KNOW these guys are going to be shooting at deer, elk, and bear with three days of practice and some pretty marginal hunting equipment. THERE IS NO WAY A BEGINNING ARCHER SHOULD ATTEMPT TO TAKE A BIG GAME ANIMAL WITH BOW AND ARROW UNTIL HE/SHE IS COMPLETELY EFFICIENT. THAT EFFICIENCY TAKES MANY MONTHS OF PRACTICE!

Today in bowhunting we even have SLOB BOWHUNTERS! There used to be no such thing! By definition, because one chose to become a bowhunter, he or she COULDN'T be a slob hunter. The slob hunter was always the LAZY hunter who would never put forth the effort necessary to become proficient at stalking, scouting, and shooting the bow. Because we made it EASY and POPULAR, we attracted the SLOB hunter into our sport. A good analogy would be to think of what happened with the advent of the four-wheel-drive truck, the trail bike, and the "four wheeler." As each was brought on the market, the number of big game hunters increased nationwide, those who joined the ranks of hunters were, by-and-large, those who wouldn't hunt before, because of the physical effort that had to be put forth in hiking, setting up a camp, and actually hunting, not to mention hauling out the elk after it was down.

I'll never forget my wife, Karen, coming home from the dentist's office one day, shaking her head in disbelief. She had mentioned to the girl who cleaned her teeth that she and her husband were bowhunters. The hygienist responded that her husband had bought a bow and really wanted to hunt but couldn't, because he didn't have the money to purchase a four-wheel-drive pickup truck. You gotta be kidding me!

In the earlier days of bowhunting, when the hunters had put in the necessary time to learn the traditions of their sport, become proficient with the bow, and had learned to stalk and scout, THE COMPETITION WAS

BETWEEN THE HUNTER AND HIMSELF AND BE-
TWEEN THE HUNTER AND THE ANIMAL. As more
and more instant bowhunters went afield, the competition began to shift to that of competition between hunters.
Who could get the biggest, the most, or do it first? It
became imperative to put a head in the record book. When
putting a head in "the book" became so important, then
people who called themselves "bowhunters" started
taking shortcuts. It is fairly common knowledge that
some of the "archery killed" heads that are registered in
the Pope and Young records were killed with firearms.The
Pope and Young Club is not responsible for this problem.
The club is composed of the most ethical bowhunters in
the world. The club has to accept a head for entry in the
record book, if the hunter claims it was bow-killed, unless
the club can prove otherwise.

The animals that we are hunting with bow and arrow
are magnificent creatures, from the seventy pound doe to
the 1,600 pound moose. They deserve our respect. THEY
SHOULD NOT BE USED AS STEPPING STONES TO
GLORY! We have bowhunters now who are trying to take
as many WORLD RECORDS as possible. They obviously don't care about the animal: they care about being
"famous." One company paid out $81,000 for their
"sponsored" bowhunter to take the grand slam of North
American Sheep with bow and arrow (Desert Big Horn
Sheep, Rocky Mountain Big Horn Sheep, Dall Sheep, and
Stone Sheep)! We have allowed the industry and the
bionic bowhunters to reduce our sport to "glory" and
"dollars and cents." Do you think that the above
mentioned bowhunter, who was essentially "hired" to
take the "grand slam," cared for those animals? I don't!
He was too busy trying to pile them up and write about his
great accomplishments in the major "sporting"
magazines. These magazines, with a very few exceptions,
are partly responsible for these goings-on, because they

"Rosey" Roseland, a top lion guide and darn good Bowhunter, with a 340 inch bull taken out of a tree stand over a wallow. This is the second consecutive bull taken over the same wallow for Rosey.

print the stories that glorify these slobs!

Gene Wensel was working on a buck one time in the Bitterroot archery area, not far from where he lived. The buck was smart, and Gene really went to work on him. It took him about three weeks to finally outsmart this old boy. (You can bet this was a SMART buck if it took someone as good as Gene that long to pattern him.) When Gene called me to tell me that he had finally taken this buck, I asked a question that, today, I no longer ask or even consider . . . (all of us have fallen into that trap at one time or another of reducing our quarry to a series of measurements) . . . I said to Gene, "Did he make the 'book'?" His answer will stay with me forever, as one of the most important lessons I have learned as a bowhunter. Gene said to me, "Hey, he made MY book!" The size of the animal means nothing compared to the way in which it was taken. There is nothing wrong with recording trophies if it is done in the right spirit, but to take an animal's life to promote an ego trip is lower than low; it is truly disgusting.

It is time for all of us, as hunters, to take the lead in sponsoring a re-kindling of awareness of the history, ethics, traditions, and fair play that was once so strongly a part of our sport. If we allow current trends to continue, we will lose bowhunting — count on it! As more unschooled hunters enter the sport of bowhunting, as more gadgetry is introduced to lessen the difficulty of bowhunting, and as more publicity is generated by manufacturers and "sporting" publications glorifying the taking of "trophy" animals, kill ratios will climb. We will see more confrontations between so-called "sportsmen" and landowners. We will see more vandalism. We will see more wounded game. Fish and Game Departments are watching these things carefully. In some states, seasons are already being shortened, because of increased hunter

The hunt is never over when you can surround yourself with memories of game fairly taken, and good times outdoors

numbers, higher "kill ratios," and game department concern about technological advances in archery.

Every one of us who cares about the future of hunting in general, and bowhunting in particular, should take the role of teacher to the newcomers to our sport. If you are using the gadgetry and supporting the companies who are gradually killing our sport, you should take a good long look at what is happening out there — maybe it's time to change — maybe it's time to boycott companies like PSE and Barnett. (These two companies are spending tens of thousands of dollars, behind the scenes, to legalize crossbows in our archery seasons. There is absolute proof that this has been done — it is not a figment of my imagination.) If you really care about bowhunting, learn about the history and traditions, get back to the basics, and place importance on using skill instead of technology to take that "critter." It proves nothing to yourself or to anyone else to shoot an animal at seventy yards using sight pins and a range finder. You will have gained my respect and will have realized a great deal of SELF-RESPECT AND SATISFACTION, if you take that animal at fifteen yards after outsmarting him and taking him in his "living room."

There is an organization out there that is called the Professional Bowhunters Society. Its membership is composed of the finest, and most responsible bowhunters in the world. Its purpose is to serve as a fraternity of dedicated, "professional" bowhunters — bowhunters who accept the task of protecting and enhancing our sport. I am very proud to be able to call myself a member of that organization. I would like to quote some comments of some PBS members. Please read and digest these comments. If you care about bowhunting, you will find some pretty "heavy" food for thought in them.

187

Gene congratulates his 12-year old son, Ken. His first day hunting he took this doe from a tree stand. One of the greatest rewards for the hunter is to bring up a new generation of bowhunters.

"A lot of people feel that we must remove the human element from bowhunting. Lord, I thought that was one of the reasons we did it. Until we change our 'success at any cost' attitude, nothing is going to change." — G. Fred Asbell, PBS member, and president of the Pope and Young Club. Fred is not only a superb hunter, but he makes a great recurve bow, "The Big Horn."

"How you take an animal and how you conduct the hunt, and what you gain from the experience is what bowhunting is all about. The value of the hunt is (or should be) proportional to the effort one puts into it." — Jay Massey, PBS member, Alaskan outfitter, author, and one of the best and most ethical bowhunters I have had the pleasure of knowing.

"If we maintain the quality of our sport, it will be here for the future generations to enjoy. That is our responsibility, yours and mine." — John Rook, PBS regular member, and Pope and Young Club member. JOHN HAS *EARNED* THE RESPECT OF BOWHUNTERS ALL OVER THE WORLD — HE IS TOTALLY *BLIND!* Because of the dedication of his friends, who hunt with him, and have developed a system of sighting and signals, John is able to bowhunt. He shoots a recurve bow and has taken many fine animals with "stick and string." He is an incredible human being, and personifies the spirit and dedication of the REAL BOWHUNTER and PBS member.

BowHUNTING is the name of our sport — it is not bowKILLING! It's very important that all of us remember that. When that big bull elk is quartering toward you and you know that it's a poor shot, but, "He'll go at least 340 P&Y!" — DON'T TAKE THAT SHOT!! There is no excuse for taking a marginal shot and risk wounding or causing a slow and agonizing death of a magnificent game animal. Anyone who would do this in order to brag and put a head on the wall doesn't deserve the title of "bowhunter." WAIT — there will be many more opportunities. You won't believe how good you feel knowing that you put a higher value on the life of that animal than on showing him off to the public. Remember what I said before: you ain't competing with other hunters — you are competing with yourself and the quarry! The limits and restrictions you place upon yourself will make you one of the elite . . . A REAL BOWHUNTER.

Keep 'em sharp and
shoot straight!

Paul Brunner
"World's Shortest Bowhunter"

Should any of my readers wish to apply for membership in the Professional Bowhunters Society, I suggest you contact our Secretary:

Jack Smith
P.O. Box 5275
Charlotte, NC 28225

The PBS publishes a super bowhunting magazine, and hosts a bowhunters convention every two years. I recommend it highly.

This is one of the best parts of the hunt; leg of venison shared with good friends who hunt and share the great outdoors together. Eat your heart out, Cleveland Amory!

For your convenience, I am listing sources of some of the hunting products that have been discussed in the book. I have tried to list companies that offer one-hundred percent guarantees on their product and are known for high quality and fair dealing.

The most frequently listed supplier is Eco Outdoor Enterprises, Inc. That is my company. I started it because I couldn't get a lot of hunting items that I wanted. My hunting partners were having the same problems. Designing and selling the Screaming Eagle Tree Stands and the "Woolie Booger" hand warmers led to other things, and our mail order catalog of "hard-to-find" outdoor items was born. We're really proud of the products we have located and designed. We have had the assistance of some of the best hunters alive in designing and testing these "goodies." We think you will like our catalog, but there are a lot of other really reliable mail order companies out there — give 'em a try!

Montana Pitch Blend Leather Dressing
"Pit Stop" Long-lasting, Natural Deodorant
ECWCS Super Heavy-duty Polypropylene
Long Underwear
ECWCS Fiber Pile Shirts and Pants
Wool Camo Balaclava Helmets
Red Ball Insulated Boots
New U.S. Army "Bunny" Boots
Tree Bark and Tiger Stripe Bandannas
"Woolie Booger" Hand Warmers
Screaming Eagle Tree Stands
Filson Wool Vests
"Bino" Shirts

All these are available from:

Eco Outdoor Enterprises, Inc.

Box 10, Ovando, Montana 59854

(406) 793-5781 (800) 458-2017

(call or write for FREE catalog)

Polar Fleece "Camo" Clothing is available in many catalogs and some stores. Eco Enterprises carries a special "Tree Stander" jacket and pants in Tree Bark™ Polar Fleece.

Hunter's Specialties Lined and Unlined Cotton Gloves with Special Grip Weave are available at almost any sporting goods store and from Eco Enterprises.

Zwickey Broadheads are available at virtually any archery shop, and some catalogs. We also carry them here at Eco Enterprises.

Hunter's Specialties Scent Wafers are available at almost any sporting goods store, and we carry them at Eco Enterprises.

Charcoal Gray Wool Pants, Main Hunting Shoes, and "Mole Skin" Pants are available from:

L. L. Bean, Inc. Freeport, Maine 04033

L. L. Bean is one of the oldest and most reliable mail order houses in the U.S. I grew up wearing their clothes and boots and was so impressed with their quality, service, and guarantee that I patterned my mail order business after them to some degree. Give 'em a try — you'll be pleased.

There are some excellent books available on whitetail deer hunting and bowhunting that will really help improve your deer hunting skills. I have read both of Gene Wensel's books on whitetails: Hunting Rutting Whitetails and One Man's Whitetail. They are the finest "how-to" books I have ever read, and I re-read them several times each year. Gene is a hunter who writes instead of a writer who hunts — there is generally a BIG difference!

Both these books can be ordered from Eco Enterprises or from Gene Wensel direct at:

Classic Whitetails Box 62 Hamilton, Montana 59840

Another great book that deals not only with hunting stories, but about the philosophies of bowhunting as well is a book called <u>A Thousand Campfires</u>, by Jay Massey. It can be ordered from Eco Enterprises or from Jay Massey direct at:

Bear Paw Publications
P.O. Box 429   Girdwood, Alaska 99587

I've also included a list of custom bow builders (bowyers) for those who are interested in finding out more about recurves and longbows. If any of my readers have questions they would like to ask me about bows, arrows, or other hunting gear, feel free to call on our business number at Eco Enterprises — don't waste your call during elk season, though!

Bruin Bows
Mike Steliga
W9664 Hwy. D
Antigo, WI 54409
715-623-6537

Bighorn Recurves
G. Fred Asbell
1340 Factory Circle
Ft. Lupton, CO 80621
303-659-0077

Cascade Bows
Steve Gorr
13008 228th NE
Arlington, WA 98223
206-435-4251

Dave Kiepert Bows
129 SW Taft
Bend, OR 97702
503-389-0586

Trails End Recurves
Dale Dye
SE 200 Grantsdale Rd.
Hamilton, MT 59840
406-363-2983

Black Widow Bows
Ken Beck
HCR #1 Box 357-1
Highlandville, MO 65669
417-587-3358

Silvertip Recurves
Paul Schafer
495 S Many Lakes Dr.
Kalispell, MT 59901
406-257-0740

Fedora Bows
Mike Fedora
RD 1 Box 151
Richland, PA 17087
717-933-8862

Assenheimer Recurves
Don Assenheimer
1005 River Rd.
Bucyrus, OH 44820

Hokolesqua Bows
Jim Emerson
2215 Friendship Dr.
New Concord, OH 43762
614-826-4688

Alan Rothhaar
7707 Gun Lake Rd.
Delton, MI 49046
616-795-3832

Plainsman Recurves
Fred Hass
P.O. Box 465
Shelby, MT 59474

Ray Young Recurves
785 Hamilton Court
Carlisle, PA 17013
717-249-2822

Heritage Bows
Rocky Miller
P.O. Box 783
Bozeman, MT 59715
406-586-5803

Jim Brakenbury
8615 SE 257th Ave.
Gresham, OR 97030
503-666-1667

Bob Savage
314 S. Grand
Bozeman, MT 59715
406-586-5803

Brigham Bows
Bob Brigham
146 Burrows St.
Geneva, OH 44041
216-466-4219

Rocky Mountain Recurves
16955 Brackett Creek Rd.
Bozeman, MT 59715
406-686-4755

Ram Bows
629 N 9th St.
Montevideo, MN 56265
612-269-6882

Don McCann
403 B. St. NE
Auburn, WA 98002

Arkansas Sticks
Terry Hughes
Rt. 1 Box 77
Gurdon, AR 71743
501-353-2032

Jack's Traditional Archery
Jack Bowers
28513 158th Ave.
East Graham, WA 98838

Rocky Mountain Archery
P.O. Box 1086
Aztec, NM 87410
505-334-9142

Cebuhar Recurves
Pat Cebuhar
785 N 7th
Canton, IL 61520

Jeffrey Archery
Owen Jeffrey
P.O. Box 9625
Columbia, SC 29290

Bighorn Longbows
Ron Maulding
P.O. Box 1857
Bozeman, MT 59715

Robertson Stykbows
Dick Robertson
P.O. Box 1432
Hamilton, MT 59840
406-363-2528

Zipper Recurves
Bob Thompson
Rt. 1, Box 147A
Ravenswood, WV 26164

Dave Johnson Bows
8213 NW 31st St.
Bethany, OK 73008
405-789-1368

Superstition Longbows
Chuck Wells
9904 N. 88th Ave.
Peoria, AZ 85345

Archery Traditions
Dan Quillan
483 W. Cloverhurst Ave.
Athens, GA 30606
404-543-1893

Don Adams Archery
24758 Warthen Rd.
Elmira, OR 97437

Pridgeon Bows
Brian Pridgeon
235 Luna
Los Lunas, NM 87031
505-865-5068

Spirit Longbows
John Strunk
5513 3rd Street
Tillamook, OR 97141
503-842-4944

Scorpion Longbows
M. R. Hamilton
Box 65
Crestone, CO 81131

J. K. Chastain Bows
490 S. Queens St.
Lakewood, CO 80226
303-989-1120

Coe Archery
Otter Lake, MI 48464

Burleson Recurves
Richard Burleson
5980 Gilbert Road
Pittsford, MI 49271

Old Timer Longbows
319 Manatawny St.
Pottstown, PA 19464

Great Northern Longbows
Rick Shepard & Jerry Brumm
8525 Thornapple Lake Rd.
Nashville, MI 49073
517-852-9340

American Longbows
John Schulz
P.O. Box 455
Cody, WY 82414

Rick's Works
6708-C MAC
Las Cruces, NM 88001

Kramer Archery
P.O. Box 62
St. Ignatius, MT 59865

Monarch Longbows
Byron Schurg
W2890 Lorraine Dr.
Missoula, MT 59803
406-251-3300

Bridgeon Longbows
9513 Snowheights NE
Albuquerque, NM 87112

Cascade Mountain Archery
Fred Anderson
E. 750 Krabbenhoft
Grapeview, WA 98546
206-426-8634

Anyan Longbows
Keith Anyan
P.O. Box 621
Ione, WA 99139

Longriver Custom Longbows
A. Gus DellaGhelfa
74 Woodbine St.
Torrington, CT 06790
203-482-1617

Carpenter Longbows
5811 Alva Ave.
Klamath Falls, OR 97603

Zebra Longbow Mfg.
Rt. 2, Box 247
Potosi, WI 53820

Texas Longbows
1211 Oak Estates
San Antonio, TX 78258

Jerry Hill Longbow Co.
P.O. Box 334
Harpersville, AL 35078
205-672-7614

Bows Unlimited
116 Veranda NW
Albuquerque, NM 87107

Stevens Takedown Recurves
1327 E. 4th
Ottumwa, IA 52501

Traditional Longbows
Frank SanMarco
RFD 5, Box 477
Watermelon Hill Road
Mahopac, NY

CV Primitives
1900 Dry Creek
Round Rock, TX 78681
512-388-4978

Bill Stewart Recurves
3701 Gun Club Road, #26
Yakima, WA 98901

**Border Custom Recurves
& Longbows**
Imported from Scotland
SNS Marketing
P.O. Box 1130
Rockville, MD 20850
301-424-5549

Dick Palmer Archery
Box 1632-T
Fayetteville, AR 72702

Richard Martin Longbows
9344 Webster Road
Clio, MI 48420
313-686-0686

Tim Meigs
113 Rice St.
Carson City, NV 89701
702-882-8121

Great Plains Bows
William Vonderhey
P.O. Box 232
Grantville, PA 17028
717-545-2031

Mountainman Longbows
John Watson
5150 Tingley Lane
Klamath Falls, OR 97601
503-883-2114

Lionheart Longbows
1 Teehey Close
Bebington, Wirral
Merseyside, England

Howard Hill Archery
248 Canyon Creek Rd.
Hamilton, MT 59840
406-363-1359

John Tangredi
193 Meadow St.
Agawam, MA 01001
413-786-0823

Bob Faufau Recurves
Rt. 1, Box 196
Ogema, WI 54459

Elberg Longbows
P.O. Box 784
Madison, IN 47250
812-273-2677

**Don Surgess
Longbows**
Angle Rock Road
Moab, UT 84532